European Security and Hybrid Threats

Zeynep Arkan

European Security and Hybrid Threats

A Narrative in the Making

palgrave
macmillan

Zeynep Arkan
Department of International Relations
Hacettepe University
Beytepe, Ankara, Türkiye

ISBN 978-3-031-86792-7 ISBN 978-3-031-86793-4 (eBook)
https://doi.org/10.1007/978-3-031-86793-4

This Palgrave Macmillan imprint is published by the registered company Springer Nature Switzerland AG.
The registered company address is: Gewerbestrasse 11, 6330 Cham, Switzerland

To Lara

Foreword

Given the current state of the world, the relationship between a general discourse of uncertainty and more specific security narratives that seek to respond to this is a fascinating one. The broader discourse that currently confronts us talks of a world of profound instability and change, ontological insecurity, existential anxiety, fragmentation, and, above all, uncertainty. Globally, the causes are multiple but are often easy to identify in the associated security discourses—arguments about geopolitical rivalries, the rise of new powers, the decline of US hegemony, Europe's uncertainty, the appeal of populism, and the crisis of democracy and new challenges like pandemics, terrorism, and cyber warfare. The last of these might be seen as part of the developing notion of 'hybrid threats', a key idea that is addressed in the following pages. If these are considered to be the troubling issues 'out there', equally troubling is the state of our knowledge and our lack of certainty. This is so widespread that it might be considered a 'condition'; indeed, in terms of the state of our knowledge, we might, following Foucault (1970), declare Uncertainty to be the new 'episteme'.

In this fascinating study Zeynep Arkan shows that despite the wider discourse of uncertainty, quite specific narratives can still flourish. Distinguishing between the two, she argues that narratives are part of wider discourses but that a study of narratives is more particularly about the structuring of stories and how this shapes our perceptions of reality. In this case, we are concerned with the framing of international politics and the sequential structure that organises events into a coherent story that enables certain forms of action. Uncertainty does not, therefore, mean inaction or indecision, even if the time is 'out of joint'. Rather, it is the very terrain on which certain narratives can prosper and gain resonance. As mentioned, recent discussion of hybrid threats is particularly prominent among these narratives, functioning as a 'leitmotif' across policy discussions, strategic frameworks, and wider political discourse.

Focusing on European security narratives, the book argues that it is precisely the multifaceted and ambiguous nature of hybrid threats that serves as a symbolic and unifying thread, giving coherence to diverse security concerns. This represents a transformation in the way that security is conceptualised by both NATO and the EU, allowing these organisations to portray themselves as defenders of the Liberal International Order (Bargués et al., 2023) and the European way of life. There is also talk of the need to show resilience in the face of adversity, and this particular concept has moved from being applied to specific things like groups, individuals, practices, and infrastructure, to the whole of society. This is particularly so following the Russian annexation of Crimea in 2014 and the ongoing Russia-Ukraine War, as well as the efforts of Russia and other authoritarian states to destabilise Western democratic institutions and processes. With Russia engaging in both traditional warfare with Ukraine and hybrid war with the rest of Europe, NATO and the EU call for a defence of democratic values, social cohesion, and cultural identity.

As discussed below, the EU has already used resilience as a way of capturing the multiple challenges faced at both individual and societal levels. The broadness and vagueness of the concept also worked as its strength since appeals to resilience could reach the ears of multiple actors without necessarily requiring the same understanding among them. As well as bringing together multiple actors, it could also be used to bring together a multitude of diverse challenges just as the narrative of hybrid threats is now doing. The following study traces the evolution of the hybrid threats narrative within NATO and the EU to inform us how it works to redefine European security. The notion of hybrid threats, like resilience, is described as an umbrella term that covers a wide range of concerns, notably cyberattacks, disinformation campaigns, and political interference, all of which contribute to a sense of insecurity that requires a response of togetherness.

This insecurity is the very basis on which NATO and the EU can present themselves as stabilising forces. It is this wider and deliberately vague discourse of uncertainty that provides the ground for very particular strategies and narratives of the EU and NATO. The EU, we know, presents itself as a distinctive normative power and guardian of particular 'European' values. NATO often frames its narrative as defending the democratic ideals of the West. Increasingly this narrative is shaped in relation to those who would disrupt or threaten these values. The dual function of these organisations is to ideologically defend these values and to strategically act in defence of the stability and integration of this community and promote unity against disruptive threats to the community from outside adversaries like Russia and China. The hybrid warfare narrative serves a clear purpose in highlighting the destructive potential of adversaries while justifying the role of those organisations deemed the guardians of security and democracy in Europe. This contributes to the wider discursive construction of 'the West' and the 'rest' with the Western community understood by its sharing of liberal values and democratic practices (Gheciu, 2019, pp. 33, 39). This can be considered a wider narrative because of the collective imagining of the Western community, while the management of internal tensions and differences within this community can be considered the task of more strategic narratives. This latter task leads in the direction of more pragmatic responses.

Over the last two decades, the concept of resilience has played a key role in providing this bridge between the defence of more general liberal ideals and practices and the need for a more realist approach that recognises an increasingly hostile and competitive environment. Resilience emphasises the need to deal with adversity through pragmatism and preparedness. The concept continues to be used, but its meaning has shifted so that while it was initially applied to individuals and communities, both NATO and the EU are turning to a more societal and more defensive approach to resilience and such things as the promotion of civil preparedness. NATO understands this as comprising three core functions: continuity of government, continuity of essential services to the population, and civil support to the military (NATO, 2024b). This is a realist or pragmatic response to a full spectrum of threats, including hybrid threats, but it is also a continued support for liberalism while recognising the unintended consequences of liberal policies such as free movement across borders.

A question for the future is whether the hybrid threats narrative will eventually take us in the direction of 'total defence'. Already we have seen how resilience has shifted from encouraging flexible adaptation and enterprise to emphasising robustness and the ability to withstand threats through means of a societal approach. Societal resilience is now linked to the promotion of a 'whole of society approach' as the best way to safeguard European security. This is now prominent in both NATO and EU strategies. This requires the population's preparedness for crisis or even war and is considered essential as a deterrent and indicates the willingness of a population to resist aggression. The promotion of total defence takes this a step further and represents an intensification of the threats and uncertainty narrative. It follows on from Russia's actions in Ukraine and is taken from the security strategies of frontline Nordic states like Finland and Sweden. It combines various actors across the civilian-military spectrum and looks at the ability of populations to cope and survive under extreme conditions, as has been seen in Ukraine. While this is not yet an EU or NATO doctrine, it is in line with the idea of societal resilience and is spreading to other EU member states.

Ironically, the success of the total defence narrative could undermine the alternative approaches discussed here. Its emphasis on comprehensiveness leaves little room for manoeuvre and undermines the more creative and open understanding of ideas like resilience. It may be that this more defensive narrative will lose its power as the situation in Ukraine changes, but what is clear is that narratives operate in complex contexts and that they must compete for attention under conditions of radical uncertainty.

Uccle, Belgium

Jonathan Joseph

References

Bargués, P., Joseph, J., & Juncos, A. E. (2023). Rescuing the liberal international order: crisis, resilience and EU security policy. *International Affairs, 99*(6), 2281–2299.

Foucault, F. (1970). *The Order of Things: An Archaeology of Human Sciences.* Tavistock.

Gheciu, A. (2019). NATO, Liberal Internationalism, and the Politics of Imagining the Western Security Community. *International Journal*, *74*(1), 32–46. https://doi.org/10.1177/0020702019834645

NATO. (2024b). *Resilience, Civil Preparedness and Article 3.* NATO. https://www.nato.int/cps/en/natohq/topics_132722.htm

Preface

The European security environment has been going through a profound transformation, particularly since the annexation of Crimea in 2014 and the onset of the Russia-Ukraine War in 2022. The relatively stable security order that existed at the end of the Cold War is now in a state of flux, dominated by an ongoing war as well as new sources and forms of threats that remain below the threshold of war. These threats are often labelled as 'hybrid threats' by security practitioners and policymakers. This umbrella term encapsulates a broad spectrum of insecurities that disrupt conventional conceptions of security and has since become a catchword in a security lexicon dominated by notions of risk, uncertainty, and vulnerabilities as well as resilience, situational awareness, strategic foresight, and rapid response, as exemplified by the European Union (EU)'s 2022 *Strategic Compass*.

The increasing prominence of hybrid threats within the EU and North Atlantic Treaty Organization (NATO) circles signals a broader transformation in the way security is conceptualised and operationalised in Europe. The salience of these threats, coupled with the imminent danger they represent, has resulted in the reform of the existing security architecture in Europe and the creation of new policy frameworks. More importantly, it has contributed to the transformation of the security narrative through references to the continuously evolving and ever-present character of threats in today's world. Such references have manifestly fuelled a heightened sense of insecurity across multiple levels in Europe. At the international level, this sense of insecurity has shaped how NATO and the EU view and address their security environments and challenges; at the state level, it has influenced national security strategies and policy choices; and at the individual level, it has permeated into the everyday lives and practices of citizens, prompting new forms of vigilance.

In response, both state and non-state actors have taken proactive measures to counteract these threats. NATO and the EU, as the two principal security actors in Europe, have intensified their cooperation and developed coordinated strategies that address hybrid threats on multiple fronts and levels. In doing so, they have carved out distinct but complementary roles and responsibilities for themselves at the collective level while also placing greater emphasis on the role of European societies and citizens. By promoting such concepts as awareness and resilience, NATO and the EU responsibilised societies and individuals to actively safeguard their own security and well-being against threats like radicalisation and disinformation. This approach, particularly emphasised by the EU, has foregrounded the idea of threats to the 'European way of life', a notion that encompasses democratic values, social cohesion, and cultural identity. By framing hybrid threats in these terms, the EU and NATO have reinforced a sense of insecurity at both the individual and the societal levels, mobilising collective efforts to defend perceived vulnerabilities. This framing has functioned not only as a means of legitimising proactive security measures but also as a way to define the boundaries of European identity against external and internal adversaries.

Through this narrative, NATO and the EU have contributed to the emergence of a symbolic divide in international politics—one that distinguishes between those actors who advocate for a rules-based international order and those who are perceived as threatening its very foundations. This divide is not merely metaphorical; it serves to position NATO and the EU as the guardians of democratic norms and stability, creating a dichotomy between the defenders of the established order and those cast as challengers. By framing challenges in terms of a binary opposition, it risks overlooking alternative perspectives to security and marginalising voices that advocate for diplomacy, systemic reform, or deeper engagement with those labelled as adversaries.

There is an ongoing debate regarding the novelty of hybrid threats, which is primarily centred around the impact of new technologies, the securitisation and weaponisation of issues such as migration or foreign direct investment, and the blurred line between war and peace, which has implications for the form, means, and law of war. Parallel to this, in recent years, many studies have focused on the operational, military, and legal aspects of hybrid threats. This book makes the case for a different approach. Rather than focusing on the similarities or differences between old and new conceptions of threats, it argues that it would be more rewarding to examine the potential sources and forms of insecurity associated with these 'known/unknown unknowns' and the novel approaches and strategies adopted to counter them. To this end, it utilises a narrative analysis framework to analyse the underlying stories that shape Europe's current security discourse and outlook. What distinguishes this approach is its focus on the narratives of security/insecurity in Europe and its exploration of how these narratives have been profoundly shaped by the *leitmotif* of hybrid threats. Through this, the study delves into the discursive power of hybrid threats and the ways in which they function as a lens through which both the EU and NATO—and, by extension, European states—interpret and respond to a complex security environment.

By tracing the evolution of hybrid threats within NATO and EU security narratives, this study aims to provide a deeper understanding of how security is being redefined in Europe today. It scrutinises how hybrid threats have become an umbrella term that encapsulates a wide range of concerns, from cyberattacks and disinformation campaigns to political interference and subversion, all of which have resulted in a persistent state of insecurity. The book explores the implications of this narrative for both the existing security architecture and the everyday lives of European citizens, who are now seen as active participants in the security structure through a 'whole-of-society' approach. Ultimately, the book argues, the crux of the matter lies in how NATO and the EU are *read* in reference to their security environment and *written* into existence as security actors.

In an era where threats are portrayed as complex, multifaceted, and rapidly evolving, it is essential to examine how this specific conceptualisation of security/insecurity might offer fresh insights into the present and future of the European security order. While acknowledging the challenges and threats to the security of Europe, this study seeks to explore the ways in which the current hybrid threat framework—one among many possible alternatives—has come to dominate NATO and the EU's security outlooks.

Vienna, Austria Zeynep Arkan

Acknowledgements

This book has been more than four years in the making, with many interruptions along the way—the most transformative and rewarding being motherhood. Throughout this long journey, I had the opportunity to engage with many individuals whose insights and support have been instrumental in shaping this work, and to whom I owe my deepest gratitude.

First, I am profoundly grateful to Jonathan Joseph, whose intellectual guidance and encouragement have continued to inspire me long after my doctoral studies. His unwavering support has been a cornerstone of my academic journey. I am equally indebted to Pınar Bilgin, who graciously stepped in as my adopted supervisor and has provided invaluable wisdom and mentorship over the years. My sincere thanks also go to Ilhan Uzgel, whose counsel and steadfast support have been invaluable in terms of both my academic work and my personal development, and to Soli Özel, whose encouragement and thought-provoking perspective have been enriching. I would like to express my heartfelt gratitude to Okan Aktan for his guidance over the years, John Maas for his helpful insights into the emergence and evolution of hybrid threats, and Isobel Cowper Coles and Vinoth Kuppan of Palgrave Macmillan for their guidance and patience with me during the publication process.

I was fortunate to find a second academic home in Vienna during my sabbatical leave from Hacettepe University, where I found the motivation and space to complete this manuscript. I am grateful to the *Österreichisches Institut für Internationale Politik* for offering me such a welcoming and energising environment. From the moment I arrived, I felt part of a vibrant intellectual community. I would like to extend special thanks to Cengiz Günay, Loïc Simonet, and Thomas Eder for their camaraderie and the many enriching conversations we shared.

To everyone who has supported me throughout this journey, whether through their guidance, friendship, or encouragement, I am profoundly thankful. My heartfelt thanks go, first and foremost, to my unwavering pillar of support and 'book deadline twin' Tuğba Bayar as well as to Özgehan Şenyuva, Sevil Dumanoğulları, Engin Sune, Göksu Uğurlu, Sören Keil, Andre Barrinha, and Sara Ramos Pinto. Whether through constructive feedback, moral support, or simply offering a listening ear, each of you has contributed to the completion of this project in meaningful ways.

None of this would have been possible without the unwavering love and support of my family. I am especially thankful to my parents, Alev and Sabih Arkan, who have been my foundation throughout this journey. Their boundless encouragement, patience, and belief in me have been my anchor through the most challenging times.

Finally, this book is dedicated to my daughter, Lara, whose arrival has profoundly changed my life. I hope that one day she will look upon this work with pride.

Competing Interests The author has no competing interests to declare that are relevant to the content of this manuscript.

Contents

Abbreviations

CFSP	Common Foreign and Security Policy
CSDP	Common Security and Defence Policy
EEAS	European External Action Service
ESS	European Security Strategy
EU	European Union
EUGS	European Union Global Strategy
GSEU	Shared Vision, Common Action: A Stronger Europe—A Global Strategy for the European Union's Foreign and Security Policy
Hybrid CoE	European Centre of Excellence for Countering Hybrid Threats
IR	International Relations
ISS	International Security Studies
NATO	North Atlantic Treaty Organization
SC	Strategic Compass for Security and Defence
SUS	Security Union Strategy
WEU	Western European Union

CHAPTER 1

Introduction

We have slain a large dragon, but we live now in a jungle filled with a bewildering variety of poisonous snakes. And, in many ways, the dragon was easier to keep track of.
James Woolsey to the United States Senate, 1993

The period that followed the end of the Cold War was a peculiar time for European security. Despite the outbreak of a series of violent conflicts in the Balkans, Europe and its nation-states were widely considered safe. During this period, often described as 'the triumph of the West' (Fukuyama, 1989), the rigid political divisions of the Cold War—splitting the world and Europe into spheres of influence dominated by the two superpowers—gave way to what appeared to be an ideal liberal world order. It was a world in which Europe was considered safe and free from direct threats as well as from great power rivalry. With the collapse of the Soviet Union, "no specific threat to the European continent, to the territorial integrity of European states, or even to their core political values" remained (Mérand et al., 2011b, p. 3). Yet, the institutional structures and mindset that had dominated the transatlantic community during the Cold War persisted, becoming even more complex. This was particularly true for the North Atlantic Treaty Organization (NATO), which had been created with the primary aim of protecting Europe by deterring the Soviet threat.

Z. Arkan, *European Security and Hybrid Threats*,
https://doi.org/10.1007/978-3-031-86793-4_1

Remarkably, the disappearance of the Soviet Union did not signal its death, as predicted by scholars such as Mearsheimer (1990) and Waltz (1993), who argued that NATO would lose its purpose and likely dissolve in the absence of its principal adversary. Instead, NATO adapted to the transformed order, redefined its objectives and mission, and welcomed new members into the transatlantic security community.

The continued relevance of NATO and its updated mission coincided with the rise of another significant actor on the European security scene—the European Union (EU). From its inception, the EU has incorporated a security dimension alongside its economic raison d'être. While the initial goal was to revive Europe's war-torn economies through coordinated action, the European Communities—the precursors of the EU—also aimed to create a zone of peace and stability where national economies and societies could flourish by making war "not merely unthinkable, but materially impossible" (Schuman Declaration, May 1950, n.d.). Despite being on the European Communities' agenda since their early days, forging a common policy and building a permanent institutional structure in the field of security proved to be a formidable challenge for the EU. The foundations of an EU-level security policy were laid with the 1992 Maastricht Treaty. Initially, the policy area had an intergovernmental modus operandi and primarily focused on non-military aspects of security. By providing "protection against the greatest external threats" through NATO, the United States facilitated its progress (Wallace, 2017, p. 80). NATO also provided the required military muscle for the security of the European neighbourhood following the Berlin Plus arrangements of 2003.[1]

It was argued that NATO's persistence and sustained relevance in the post-Cold War era could be attributed to several external and intra-alliance factors. These include external threats and dangers that justified its continued existence, its capacity for institutional adaptation, and "the valuable

[1] The Berlin Plus agreement of 2003 is a cooperative framework between NATO and the EU, allowing the EU to utilise NATO's assets and capabilities for crisis management operations. Under this arrangement, the EU can only proceed with using NATO resources if NATO opts not to intervene directly in a given crisis. This agreement exemplifies a commitment to resource-sharing and strategic collaboration, ensuring that the EU has the means to engage in security operations when necessary but without duplicating NATO's efforts. Ultimately, Berlin Plus arrangements facilitate operational support and complement both organisations' broader security roles within the European security architecture.

intra-alliance functions that the alliance has always performed and that remain relevant after the cold war" (Duffield, 1994, pp. 766–767) despite the disappearance of the greatest existential threat. NATO's first post-Cold War security concept noted that, in the aftermath of the Cold War, challenges and risks to the security of Europe were of a different nature than those of the past; "less likely to result from calculated aggression against the territory of the Allies, but rather from the adverse consequences of instabilities that may arise from the serious economic, social and political difficulties, including ethnic rivalries and territorial disputes" (NATO, 1991). The implication of this was a reformulation of the role and responsibilities of NATO in an environment where security risks became "multi-faceted in nature and multi-directional" (NATO, 1991). As a response, NATO opted for a broader approach to security through civilian as well as military means to complement its focus on collective defence and deterrence. By adapting its outlook, goals, and mission to the changing dynamics of the post-Cold War order, NATO upheld its central role and position within the European security architecture.

A parallel, and in many ways, purpose-driven and teleological reading of the EU's gradual evolution into a security actor is also possible. One might argue that given the changing reality of Europe following the collapse of the Berlin Wall, European states had little choice but to expand their zone of stability and prosperity while simultaneously laying the foundations for more institutionalised cooperation in foreign and security policy. Many commentators have also stated that the EU needed to balance its economic clout with a foreign policy dimension to better project its political influence on both regional and global levels. The former Belgian Foreign Minister Mark Eyskens' description of Europe as "an economic giant, a political dwarf, and a military worm" is often cited to support this argument (as quoted in Whitney, 1991). The burgeoning role of the EU as a security actor is then rationalised through a collective political will to lessen Europe's reliance on the United States for its security needs and for Europeans to be able to protect themselves and secure their neighbourhood in the face of present and emergent threats, including "nontraditional security threats such as failed states and transnational organized crime" (Merlingen, 2012, p. 32). It is often noted that though the European political will proved strong enough to establish a legal framework for a Common Foreign and Security Policy (CFSP) in 1992, this achievement did not prevent the EU from facing humiliation during the

Balkan conflicts. Despite occurring in its own backyard, the EU, in fact, failed to bring an end to the violence, accentuating a significant disparity between its capabilities and the expectations placed upon it. This shortcoming further substantiated the argument that "the Community is not an effective international actor, in terms both of its capacity to produce collective decisions and its impact on events" (Hill, 1993, p. 306). Such a conspicuous failure on the part of the EU and its member states spurred a wave of change in the Union's outlook and commitments in the field of security and ultimately led to the EU's progressive absorption of the Western European Union (WEU) and the strengthening of the CFSP and the Common Security and Defence Policy (CSDP).

Locating NATO and the EU Within the European Security Landscape: A Theoretical Overview

To what extent the evolution of the roles and responsibilities of NATO and the EU in the post-Cold War security environment can be explained by particular internal and/or external dynamics is a complex question that invites a range of theoretical perspectives from International Relations (IR) and International Security Studies (ISS) standpoints. Each perspective offers a distinct set of assumptions, key concepts, and explanatory tools that inform the analysis, methods adopted, and conclusions drawn. They also offer diverse stories about the world of international politics, its key actors, and dynamics. "And in telling stories about international politics", they do not just mirror the 'reality' of international politics; they also impose their "own vision of what the world out there looks like" (Weber, 2010, p. 2).

This study contributes to these debates by adopting a critical approach to examine the narratives that structure the discourse on European security. Drawing on a poststructuralist framework infused with narrative analysis, it interrogates how NATO and the EU construct security, articulate threats, position themselves, and legitimise their respective responses. By placing narratives at the centre of its analysis, this approach seeks to uncover the power dynamics and political assumptions that underpin these constructs, offering an alternative lens through which to understand the current debates on European security.

Another story, however, would be told by the realist school of IR. From a realist perspective, the analysis would likely centre on the distribution of power and the enduring relevance of state interests (Waltz, 1979). Realists would argue that NATO's persistence and the EU's expanded security role can be seen as responses to shifting power balances within the international system. They may focus specifically on the renewed threat of a resurgent Russia or the rise of non-state actors, which would push European states to prioritise collective action (Schweller & Priess, 1997). For realists, the survival and adaptability of NATO and the EU in security affairs are attributed to the pragmatic need for power balancing and the maintenance of state sovereignty within an anarchic global system (Mearsheimer, 2001). A prime example of this is the work of Hyde-Price, who applies realist insights to European security in the aftermath of the Cold War and the key role played by EU member states in the integration process (2013). Exploring the dynamics of security competition as well as cooperation among European states, he makes a case for a 'balanced multipolar' reading of the existing security order, which goes against the common understanding of Europe as 'a Kantian paradise' of prosperity and peace (Hyde-Price, 2006, 2007).

In contrast, a liberal approach would highlight the role of institutions, interdependence, and shared democratic values in shaping NATO and the EU's post-Cold War security functions. This literature also includes the works of neofunctionalist scholars that centre around the progressive logic of spillovers (Niemann, 2006). Liberals would argue that these organisations have evolved not merely out of necessity but due to the absolute gains they provide, such as reducing transaction costs, increasing transparency, and building trust among member states (Keohane & Nye, 1977), as well as national economic interests (Moravcsik, 1998). The EU's security initiatives, such as the CSDP, might be rationalised as extensions of Europe's commitment to fostering a liberal, rules-based order (Schimmelfennig, 2003), one in which collective action is seen as essential to tackling shared threats (Wagner, 2017). NATO's endurance and the EU's complementary security role would thus be viewed as products of institutionalised cooperation among democracies (Wallander, 2000), aimed at maintaining stability and promoting shared norms (Tocci, 2021).

A constructivist or poststructuralist take on the same question would offer radically different accounts, focusing instead on how ideas, identities, shared beliefs, and discourses influence NATO and the EU's evolving roles and responsibilities (Checkel & Katzenstein, 2009; Derrida, 1992; Diez, 2001; Hansen & Wæver, 2002). Constructivists would argue that conceptions of security and insecurity in Europe are socially constituted, shaped by historical experiences, interactions, and evolving identities (Wendt, 1994). They would explore how NATO and the EU redefine their purposes in response to shifts in collective identity and representations of threat (Kınacıoğlu & Gürzel, 2013). Constructivists would attribute the shift in NATO's role over the years from a defensive alliance to one that embraces broader security concerns to the transformation of its identity as well as interests (Gheciu, 2005). Checkel (2005) adds to this by examining how institutions like NATO and the EU socialise member states into shared norms.

A poststructuralist approach, on the other hand, would delve deeper into the ways in which NATO and the EU's identities are constituted, emphasising that security is not an objective or fixed reality but rather a notion produced and reproduced through discourse and embedded in power relations (Campbell, 1998). Poststructuralists would argue that the discourse surrounding Europe and its security is shaped by specific discursive practices that serve to accentuate the positions of certain actors and marginalise others (L. Hansen, 2006). For instance, by framing NATO as a 'defender of democracy' or the EU as a 'stabilising force', dominant discourses create a reality in which these organisations are perceived as inherently positive and necessary, obscuring alternative interpretations. Poststructuralist analyses also shed light on how NATO functions as a "set of practices by which the West has constituted itself as a political and cultural entity" (Klein, 1990, p. 311). Such framing also creates certain 'Others'—such as Russia or specific non-state actors—as threats, which justifies the expansion and militarisation of European security measures (Libiseller, 2023; Mälksoo, 2018). From a poststructuralist standpoint, the EU's emergence as a security actor can be seen as part of a broader shift in the discourse on European integration, where security becomes intertwined with the preservation of a particular conception of European identity, symbolising both unity and independence from external pressures (Eberle & Daniel, 2022).

Finally, Marxist or postcolonial approaches would take yet another route, questioning the deeper power structures and inequalities that shape the global order. The former would interpret the exercise and expansion of American power as a mechanism for securing capitalist interests, both within Europe and on a global scale (Cox, 1981), shaped by various factors, including "the historically specific ways in which mass production was institutionalized, and by the political, cultural, and ideological aspects of this process at home and abroad" (Rupert, 1995, p. 2). NATO's and the EU's engagement in security matters would be viewed as serving economic elites by stabilising regions crucial for trade, investment, or energy supply (Overbeek & Apeldoorn, 2012). Postcolonial scholars, on the other hand, might argue that NATO and the EU's interventions reflect a continuation of Western dominance and a tendency to impose Western security norms on non-Western states (Linklater, 1998). These critical perspectives challenge mainstream understandings by exposing underlying power asymmetries as well as the continued impact of Europe's colonial legacy, questioning the legitimacy of the Western-centric security order promoted by NATO and the EU (Hoijtink et al., 2023; Fisher-Onar, 2023; Sachseder & Stachowitsch, 2023).

The main contribution of critical approaches has been to challenge the dominant frameworks of conventional theories by exposing their implicit underlying assumptions. Through this, they have shifted the centre of gravity in the discipline of IR by introducing a sense of doubt—doubt about the epistemological as well as empirical assumptions of the study of international relations as well as its ontological position (Wyn Jones, 2001). Realist and liberal theories often treat key concepts such as sovereignty, power, order, and security as objective givens shaped by material conditions or institutional arrangements. In contrast, critical perspectives, particularly the poststructuralist one, argue that these are not simply observed but constituted through social practices. By shifting the centre of gravity, critical theories provide a richer understanding of the evolving roles and responsibilities of NATO and the EU in shaping the European security environment.

A complementary analysis from the standpoint of ISS provides additional perspectives into the security functions of NATO and the EU. Where contemporary IR theories emphasise concepts such as power, institutions, and ideas, ISS expands the analytical framework to include a broader array of threats and challenges, focusing on how these are managed by different actors, including states and international organisations. The field of ISS provides a multifaceted understanding of NATO and the EU's evolving functions in European security by offering insights into how these organisations navigate a complex security environment marked by both traditional military threats and emerging non-military challenges.

Traditional security approaches, which "has been associated with the intellectual hegemony of realism" (Booth, 1991, p. 318), view NATO as an indispensable military alliance whose primary function is the collective defence of its member states. During the Cold War era, this implied "maintaining a credible force capability, both in conventional and nuclear terms, to deter large-scale armed attack and to defend national territory in the event of war" for NATO members (Barrett, 1996, p. 123). In today's security environment, characterised by a resurgent Russia and escalating great power competition, scholars would argue that NATO's enduring focus on deterrence and military preparedness remains vital and that "the umbilical security cord across the Atlantic" (Sloan, 1986, p. 127) should be preserved. The deployment of NATO forces to Eastern Europe and the modernisation of its defence posture are interpreted as pragmatic responses to tangible state-based threats. While the EU would not be considered a hard security actor within this framework, the traditional security literature would acknowledge the bloc's efforts to bolster resilience against current threats, such as cyberattacks and disinformation campaigns, even if these measures are seen as supplementary to NATO's military capabilities. As it is often noted, "NATO and the EU play complementary, coherent and mutually reinforcing roles in supporting international peace and security", and these include cooperation to counter threats of a hybrid nature (NATO, 2024b). Yet, it is also deemed vital for the EU to be prepared to proactively defend its own interests in what appears to be a fragmented multipolar world order (Biscop, 2024). Echoing the words of Jacques Delors, the former President of the European Commission, Biscop, underlines that it is vital for Europeans to recognise that "[i]nternational politics is not about charity" and humanitarian aid does not equal foreign policy (2018, p. 1).

It is claimed that "[t]he strongest blow to orthodox security studies was dealt on the European ring, almost single-handedly by the end of the Cold War" (Mérand et al., 2011a, p. 12). Towards the end of the Cold War era, "the seeds were sown for a new conception of security" (Barrett, 1996, p. 123) and the field of ISS significantly broadened, recognising that security threats now extend far beyond conventional military, state-focused dangers. Deemed "inadequate to the task of accounting for a new landscape of security issues and actors", traditional approaches to security lost their privileged position and new approaches emerged that offered new categories of thought (Burgess, 2012, p. 2). The broadening and deepening of security and the approaches associated with such intellectual opening aimed to address non-traditional challenges, such as climate change, economic instability, and public health crises, through a critical lens (Buzan et al., 1998). Scholars adopting such perspectives explored NATO's adaptation to address these evolving threats, such as its initiatives in counterterrorism and disaster response. Similarly, the EU's security role became far more pronounced within the expanded security framework. Its initiatives in climate security, crisis management, and the protection of digital infrastructure are viewed as essential contributions to a comprehensive European security architecture (Council of the European Union, 2022). The COVID-19 pandemic, climate-induced migration, and the vulnerabilities of global supply chains are construed as reminders of the interconnectedness of contemporary security threats (Tocci, 2021), reinforcing the necessity for NATO and the EU to adopt comprehensive, coordinated strategies (NATO, 2024b).

Securitisation theory, a cornerstone of critical security studies, adds another layer of analysis by examining how specific issues are constructed as security threats through speech acts (Wæver, 1989, 1995; Buzan et al., 1998). Central to this theory is the idea that security is not an objective condition but a linguistic practice, wherein political actors elevate specific issues to the status of threats, thereby legitimising extraordinary measures outside the bounds of normal politics. NATO's narrative of defending democracy and countering Russian aggression exemplifies this process, as it frames geopolitical adversaries and hybrid threats in ways that justify heightened military spending, expanded defence postures, and collective security measures. The EU's framing of migration as a security crisis similarly illustrates how political actors can securitise social and economic phenomena to justify extraordinary policies, such as enhanced border controls and restrictive asylum measures.

New avenues for research are further opened following a redefinition of the concept of securitisation to include contextual factors such as audience reception and sociopolitical structures in determining the success of securitisation processes. In "A Theory of Securitisation", Balzacq notes that "securitization consists of practices which instantiate *intersubjective* understandings through the *habitus* inherited from different, often competing social fields" (2011, p. 2). This expanded perspective offers a more nuanced understanding of how threats are received by the audience and made actionable, demonstrating the ways in which securitisation operates as a political tool to mobilise resources and enact specific policy agendas as well as extraordinary measures. The inherent connection between these measures, practices, and discourse as a meaning-making exercise has influenced other works that utilised the concept of securitisation that went beyond the confines of speech acts (Huysmans, 2006). This was part of a greater turn towards discursive influences and non-positivist methodologies within the broad framework of critical security studies, which also includes contributions from feminist, critical security studies, and postcolonial scholars. These approaches collectively challenge the depoliticisation and normalisation of security practices, calling for greater scrutiny of their ethical and political implications. An obvious case of this is the framing of migration as a security crisis that shifts the debate from humanitarian responsibility to border control and surveillance, effectively normalising exclusionary practices (Huysmans, 2006). A similar dynamic is evident in the case of NATO and the EU's responses to the changing security environment and their increasing emphasis on such notions as resilience against evolving and unpredictable challenges (NATO, 2024a; European Commission, 2020). NATO's narrative of defending democracy and countering Russian aggression frequently invokes hybrid threats as existential challenges, thereby justifying heightened military spending and collective defence measures. Meanwhile, the EU's framing of resilience against hybrid threats positions it as a multidimensional actor capable of addressing vulnerabilities in diverse spheres, including digital infrastructure, economic interdependence, and governance. These narratives not only shape institutional practices but also influence how European security is perceived and prioritised, often reinforcing Western-centric frameworks, while marginalising alternative perspectives, such as human security or conflict prevention.

A critical analysis of the dynamics involved in the conceptualisation and operationalisation of the current European security order uncovers the power relations underpinning NATO's and the EU's roles within the security architecture. A comprehensive framework that facilitates such analysis is the poststructuralist perspective on security, which views security not as an objective or protective function but as a power that constitutes subjects, spaces, and hierarchies and "interrogate[s] security as a form of productive power that makes reality intelligible and actionable in particular ways" (Aradau & van Munster, 2018, p. 75). By focusing on the performative and constitutive dimensions of security practices, poststructuralist scholars explore how discourses of security/insecurity bring particular threats and identities into being while marginalising others, thereby shaping the parameters of political action. Through this perspective, security is transformed into "an ontological double requirement": the polity in question "needed to be secure, but it also needed the threatening Other to define its identity, thereby giving it ontological security" (Buzan & Hansen, 2009, p. 218).

The gradual emergence of critical approaches within ISS followed the same logic that critical IR perspectives did, leading to the questioning of both the unit of analysis and the underlying epistemological and ontological assumptions regarding objective/subjective understandings of the concept of security. The different theoretical perspectives under both IR and ISS underscore the multiplicity of possible explanations for understanding NATO and the EU's evolving security functions. Each framework highlights distinct key concepts—such as power, institutions, identity, discourse, speech-acts, hierarchy, or economic structures—and offers unique interpretations of the context and drivers of these organisations' actions at various levels. Even when these perspectives operate on similar levels of analysis, their epistemological and ontological foundations differ considerably.[2] For example, *structural constraints* influencing NATO or the EU's foreign policy choices might manifest as hegemonic discursive structures or the imperatives of the international system. Each interpretation yields a different understanding of agency and the processes through which threats are conceptualised and addressed. Researchers may also seek to establish *causal* relationships or *correlations* between actors' attributes—such as identity, role perceptions/prescriptions, interests, or liberal democratic values—and specific policy actions. Ultimately, there may be more than one explanation or a combination of factors behind particular policy decisions. A comprehensive analysis might require synthesising insights from multiple approaches for the researcher to gain a more nuanced understanding of why NATO remains relevant and how the EU has come to embrace a more active role within the current security environment.

In the spirit of synthesis, this study adopts a critical lens to explore the narratives shaping the discourse on European security, bridging the theoretical depth of a poststructuralist framework with the analytical precision of narrative analysis. This integration addresses the limitations of traditional approaches, which often reduce security dynamics to static or siloed categories of threats. By leveraging poststructuralism's emphasis on the performative and constitutive dimensions of security practices, alongside narrative analysis's capacity to dissect the structure, repetition, and evolution of meaning, this study illuminates the intricate ways in which security

[2] These types of questions are of particular interest to Foreign Policy Analysis as a subdiscipline of International Relations. For more information regarding these different levels of analysis as well as the distinction between a unit of analysis and levels of analysis, see Singer (1961), Yurdusev (1993).

is constructed, contested, and operationalised. Such a synthesis is vital for capturing the complexity of contemporary security challenges, which seem to defy conventional boundaries between military and non-military domains, internal and external pressures, and war and peace. At the heart of this analysis lies the notion of hybrid threats—a recurring theme that not only underscores the ambiguity and complexity of the current security environment but also serves as a pivotal construct in shaping how institutions like NATO and the EU interpret, frame, and respond to evolving security challenges.

Echoing the inherent distinction between 'why' and 'how possible' questions (Doty, 1993), this study argues that it was not due to a set of internal or external givens that NATO maintained its central position in the European security environment in the aftermath of the Cold War, accompanied by the EU as a budding security actor. Instead, the transformation of NATO's mission and outlook, the emergence of the EU as a security community, and the development of close ties between NATO and the EU were *made possible* through a specific narrative framework. This framework enabled political leaders and experts on European security to make sense of and navigate the changing security landscape. It also provided a lens through which the roles and positions of both NATO and the EU were defined in the European security environment vis-à-vis the nation-state and other actors, in relation to a particular set of insecurities. Hybrid threats, which encompass an ever-expanding range of conventional challenges that defy traditional distinctions of war and peace, emerged as a central organising theme—a *leitmotif*—in the narrative framework on European security, shaping how insecurities are defined and addressed both by NATO and by the EU. These threats not only shape how security/insecurity is interpreted but also reflect broader struggles over the conceptualisation of Europe and the European order. By focusing on hybrid threats as discursive constructs, this study interrogates the power dynamics and political assumptions embedded in these narratives and explores their role in legitimising institutional authority and guiding policy responses.

Structurally, the book is divided into three main sections. Following this general introduction to the topic, Chap. 2 lays the theoretical foundations and outlines the method used. It explains the poststructuralist approach to security, highlights the complementary role of narrative analysis, and introduces the leitmotif of hybrid threats as a central element shaping narratives on European security. This section also examines how narratives construct meanings, identities, and threat perceptions, thereby shaping the contours of European security. Chapter 3 provides an empirical analysis of the narratives on European security, tracing the evolution of NATO and EU's security practices through a narrative lens, with particular emphasis on the framing of hybrid threats. It explores how the leitmotif of hybrid threats has influenced current discussions on European security and positioned the key protagonists—NATO, the EU, and their affiliated institutions—within the security environment, through an analysis of the three core components of security narratives: setting, characterisation, and emplotment. The book concludes by reflecting on the implications of these narratives for a particular conceptualisation of Europe and the European security order and its institutional dynamics. It offers a critical re-evaluation of the contemporary European security environment, highlighting its discursive underpinnings and the ways in which these security narratives shape policy and identity.

Bibliography

Aradau, C., & van Munster, R. (2018). Poststructuralist Approaches to Security. In M. Dunn Cavelty & T. Balzacq (Eds.), *Routledge Handbook of Security Studies* (2nd ed., pp. 75–84). Routledge.

Balzacq, T. (2011). A theory of Securitization: Origins, Core Assumptions, and variants. In T. Balzacq (Ed.), *Securitization Theory: How Security Problems Emerge and Dissolve* (pp. 1–30). Routledge.

Barrett, J. (1996). NATO Reform: Alliance Policy and Co-Operative Security. In I. Peters (Ed.), *New Security Challenges: The Adaptation of International Institutions, Reforming the UN, NATO, EU and CSCE since 1989* (pp. 123–151). St. Martin's Press.

Biscop, S. (2018). *European Strategy in the 21st Century: New Future for Old Power*. Routledge. https://doi.org/10.4324/9780429427442

Biscop, S. (2024). *EU Strategy 2025–2029: We Have the Instruments, Now Set the Objectives* (367; Egmont Policy Brief). Royal Institute for International Relations.

Booth, K. (1991). Security and Emancipation. *Review of International Studies, 17*(4), 313–326.

Burgess, J. P. (2012). Introduction. In J. P. Burgess (Ed.), *The Routledge Handbook of New Security Studies* (pp. 1–4). Routledge.

Buzan, B., & Hansen, L. (2009). *The Evolution of International Security Studies*. Cambridge University Press.

Buzan, B., Wæver, O., & Wilde, J. d. (1998). *Security: A New Framework for Analysis.* Lynne Rienner.

Campbell, D. (1998). *Writing Security: United States Foreign Policy and the Politics of Identity.* University of Minnesota Press.

Checkel, J. T. (2005). International Institutions and Socialization in Europe: Introduction and Framework. *International Organization, 59*(4), 801–826.

Checkel, J. T., & Katzenstein, P. J. (Eds.). (2009). *European Identity.* Cambridge University Press. https://doi.org/10.1017/CBO9780511806247

Council of the European Union. (2022). *A Strategic Compass for Security and Defence—For a European Union that protects its Citizens, Values and Interests and Contributes to International Peace and Security* (7371/22). https://data.consilium.europa.eu/doc/document/ST-7371-2022-INIT/en/pdf

Cox, R. W. (1981). Social Forces, States and World Orders: Beyond International Relations Theory. *Millennium: Journal of International Studies, 10*(2), 126–155. https://doi.org/10.1177/03058298810100020501

Derrida, J. (1992). *The Other Heading: Reflections on Today's Europe* (P. A. Brault & M. B. Naas, Trans.). Indiana University Press.

Diez, T. (2001). Europe as a Discursive Battleground: Discourse Analysis and European Integration Studies. *Cooperation and Conflict, 36*(1), 5–38.

Doty, R. L. (1993). Foreign Policy as Social Construction: A Post-Positivist Analysis of U.S. Counterinsurgency Policy in the Philippines. *International Studies Quarterly, 37*(3), 297–320. https://doi.org/10.2307/2600810

Duffield, J. S. (1994). NATO's Functions after the Cold War. *Political Science Quarterly, 109*(5), 763–787. https://doi.org/10.2307/2152531

Eberle, J., & Daniel, J. (2022). Anxiety Geopolitics: Hybrid Warfare, Civilisational Geopolitics, and the Janus-faced Politics of Anxiety. *Political Geography, 92*(1), 102502. https://doi.org/10.1016/j.polgeo.2021.102502

European Commission. (2020). *2020 Strategic Foresight Report—Charting the Course towards a More Resilient Europe.*

Fisher-Onar, N. (2023). Beyond Binaries: (European) Security in Feminist and Postcolonial Perspective. *European Security, 32*(3), 508–518. https://doi.org/10.1080/09662839.2023.2233436

Fukuyama, F. (1989). The End of History? *The National Interest, 16*, 3–18.

Gheciu, A. (2005). Security Institutions as Agents of Socialization? NATO and the 'New Europe'. *International Organization, 59*(4), 973–1012. https://doi.org/10.1017/S0020818305050332

Hansen, L. (2006). *Security as Practice: Discourse Analysis and the Bosnian War.* Routledge.

Hansen, L., & Wæver, O. (Eds.). (2002). *European Integration and National Identity: The Challenge of the Nordic States.* Routledge.

Hill, C. (1993). The Capability-Expectations Gap, or Conceptualizing Europe's International Role. *JCMS: Journal of Common Market Studies, 31*(3), 305–328. https://doi.org/10.1111/j.1468-5965.1993.tb00466.x

Hoijtink, M., Mühlenhoff, H. L., & Welfens, N. (2023). Whose (in)Security? Gender, Race and Coloniality in European Security Policies: Introduction to the Special Issue. *European Security, 32*(3), 335–346. https://doi.org/10.1080/09662839.2023.2235286

Huysmans, J. (2006). *The Politics of Insecurity: Fear, Migration and Asylum in the EU.* Routledge.

Hyde-Price, A. (2006). 'Normative' Power Europe: A Realist Critique. *Journal of European Public Policy, 13*(2), 217–234. https://doi.org/10.1080/13501760500451634

Hyde-Price, A. (2007). *European Security in the Twenty-first Century: The Challenge of Multipolarity.* Routledge.

Hyde-Price, A. (2013). Realism: A Dissident Voice in the Study of the CSDP. In S. Biscop & R. G. Whitman (Eds.), *The Routledge Handbook of European Security* (pp. 18–27). Routledge.

Keohane, R. O., & Nye, J. S. (1977). *Power and Interdependence: World Politics in Transition.* Little.

Kınacıoğlu, M., & Gürzel, A. G. (2013). Turkey's Contribution to NATO's Role in Post-Cold War Security Governance: The Use of Force and Security Identity Formation. *Global Governance, 19*(4), 589–610. https://doi.org/10.1163/19426720-01904007

Klein, B. S. (1990). How the West was One: Representational Politics of NATO. *International Studies Quarterly, 34*(3), 311–325. https://doi.org/10.2307/2600572

Libiseller, C. (2023). 'Hybrid Warfare' as an Academic Fashion. *Journal of Strategic Studies, 46*(4), 858–880. https://doi.org/10.1080/01402390.2023.2177987

Linklater, A. (1998). *Transformation of Political Community: Ethical Foundations of the Post-Westphalian Era.* Polity.

Mälksoo, M. (2018). Countering Hybrid Warfare as Ontological Security Management: The Emerging Practices of the EU and NATO. *European Security, 27*(3), 374–392. https://doi.org/10.1080/09662839.2018.1497984

Mearsheimer, J. J. (1990). Back to the Future: Instability in Europe after the Cold War. *International Security, 15*(1), 5–56. https://doi.org/10.2307/2538981

Mearsheimer, J. J. (2001). *The Tragedy of Great Power Politics.* W.W. Norton & Company.

Mérand, F., Foucault, M., & Irondelle, B. (Eds.). (2011a). *European Security since the Fall of the Berlin Wall.* University of Toronto Press.

Mérand, F., Irondelle, B., & Foucault, M. (2011b). Theorizing Change in the European Security Environment. In *European Security since the Fall of the Berlin Wall* (pp. 3–22). University of Toronto Press.

Merlingen, M. (2012). *EU Security Policy: What It Is, How It Works, Why It Matters.* Lynne Rienner.

Moravcsik, A. (1998). *The Choice for Europe: Social Purpose and State Power from Messina to Maastricht* (0th ed.). Routledge. https://doi.org/10.4324/9781315072258

NATO. (1991). *The Alliance's New Strategic Concept (1991)*. NATO. https://www.nato.int/cps/en/natohq/official_texts_23847.htm

NATO. (2024a). *Resilience, Civil Preparedness and Article 3*. NATO. https://www.nato.int/cps/en/natohq/topics_132722.htm

NATO. (2024b, October 3). *Relations with the European Union*. https://www.nato.int/cps/en/natohq/topics_49217.htm#:~:text=NATO%20and%20the%20EU%20play,contributes%20to%20transatlantic%20burden%2Dsharing.

Niemann, A. (2006). *Explaining Decisions in the European Union*. Cambridge University Press. https://doi.org/10.1017/CBO9780511492044

Overbeek, H., & Apeldoorn, B. v. (Eds.). (2012). *Neoliberalism in Crisis*. Palgrave Macmillan.

Rupert, M. (1995). *Producing Hegemony: The Politics of Mass Production and American Global Power*. Cambridge University Press.

Sachseder, J., & Stachowitsch, S. (2023). Gendering EU Security Strategies: A Feminist Postcolonial Approach to the EU as a (global) Security Actor. *European Security, 32*(3), 404–424. https://doi.org/10.1080/09662839.2023.2232742

Schimmelfennig, F. (2003). *The EU, NATO and the Integration of Europe: Rules and Rhetoric*. Cambridge University Press.

Schuman Declaration, May 1950 (n.d.). History of the EU - 1945–59 - Schuman Declaration May 1950. https://europeanunion.europa.eu/principles-countries-history/history-eu/1945-59/schuman-declaration-may-1950_en

Schweller, R. L., & Priess, D. (1997). A Tale of Two Realisms: Expanding the Institutions Debate. *Mershon International Studies Review, 41*(1), 1–32.

Singer, J. D. (1961). The Level-of-Analysis Problem in International Relations. *World Politics, 14*(1), 77–92. https://doi.org/10.2307/2009557

Sloan, S. R. (1986). *NATO's Future: Towards a New Transatlantic Bargain*. Macmillan Press. https://doi.org/10.1007/978-1-349-08362-6

Tocci, N. (with Istituto Affari Internazionali). (2021). *European Strategic Autonomy: What It Is, Why We Need It, How to Achieve It*. Istituto Affari Internazionali (IAI).

Wæver, O. (1989). *Security and the Speech Act: Analysing the Politics of a Word* (Working Paper No. 1989/19). Centre for Peace and Conflict Research.

Wæver, O. (1995). Securitization and Desecuritization. In R. D. Lipschutz (Ed.), *On Security* (pp. 46–86). Columbia University Press.

Wagner, W. (2017). Liberal Power Europe. *JCMS. Journal of Common Market Studies, 55*(6), 1398–1414. https://doi.org/10.1111/jcms.12572

Wallace, W. (2017). European Foreign Policy Since the Cold War: How Ambitious, How Inhibited? *The British Journal of Politics and International Relations, 19*(1), 77–90. https://doi.org/10.1177/1369148116685297
Wallander, C. A. (2000). Institutional Assets and Adaptability: NATO After the Cold War. *International Organization, 54*(4), 705–735. https://doi.org/10.1162/002081800551343
Waltz, K. N. (1979). *Theory of International Politics.* Addison-Wesley.
Waltz, K. N. (1993). The Emerging Structure of International Politics. *International Security, 18*(2), 44–79.
Weber, C. (2010). *International Relations Theory: A Critical Introduction* (3rd ed.). Routledge.
Wendt, A. (1994). Collective Identity Formation and the International State. *American Political Science Review, 88*(2), 384–396. https://doi.org/10.2307/2944711
Whitney, C. R. (1991, January 25). War in the Gulf: Europe; Gulf Fighting Shatters Europeans' Fragile Unity. *The New York Times.*
Wyn Jones, R. (2001). Introduction: Locating Critical International Relations Theory. In R. Wyn Jones (Ed.), *Critical Theory and International Politics* (pp. 1–19). Lynne Rienner.
Yurdusev, A. N. (1993). 'Level of Analysis' and 'Unit of Analysis': A Case for Distinction. *Millennium: Journal of International Studies, 22*(1), 77–88. https://doi.org/10.1177/03058298930220010601

CHAPTER 2

Narrative Analysis and Security Studies

Undertaking a critique involves an intervention or series of interventions in established modes of thought and action. Such interventions are thus positioned in a particular relationship to those practices they wish to critique. They involve an effort to disturb those practices that are settled, untie what appears to be sewn up, and render as produced that which claims to be naturally emergent. … Intervening necessarily involves a questioning of that which is established, and that questioning betrays a concern or dissatisfaction with what is settled and creates the conditions of possibility for the formulation of alternatives.
David Campbell in *National Deconstruction,* 1998

While hybrid threats form the central theme of the study, this book is not on hybrid threats per se. Nor does it seek to investigate their root causes, origins, target domains, or direct policy implications with the aim of establishing causal relationships between them. Instead, echoing Campbell (1998a, p. x), this book examines what might be termed 'metahybrid threats': the practices through which hybrid threats come into being and are rendered intelligible as security concerns, and what they do (Weldes et al., 1999). Central to this exploration are the actors involved, the political outlooks they promote, and the policy options they legitimise through their meaning-making practices. Subsequently, rather than assuming

Z. Arkan, *European Security and Hybrid Threats,*
https://doi.org/10.1007/978-3-031-86793-4_2

hybrid threats pose an inherent risk to societies or polities, this book critically interrogates the processes through which they are interpreted as such—an interpretation that is contingent, contested, and one among many.

In the preface to *Writing Security*, Campbell observes that disorienting transformations in the existing order often provoke assertions that ambiguity itself constitutes a threat, accompanied by calls to address emergent threats that "imperil settled modes of life" through an ever-expanding definition of security (1998b, p. iiv). Campbell contends that the persistent impulse to 'rethink security' serves as a reminder of the inherent fluidity shaping our political landscapes—past, present, and future (1998b, p. iiv). Representations of danger, which remain constant, reflect this fluidity by continuously adapting to shifting contexts and evolving understandings of threats. This is a dynamic process in which security/insecurity, the security environment/order, the actors in it, and their appropriate/legitimate responses are continually redefined.

As the dynamics of the present security environment in Europe illustrate, the desire to rethink security continues to be a salient response two and a half decades after the publication of Campbell's work. Amidst ongoing challenges posed by both conventional and non-conventional threats to European security, this rethinking involves not only addressing substantive issues but also engaging in critical theoretical reflection.

From a theoretical perspective, rethinking security involves grappling with fundamental questions: What constitutes a threat? How are threats identified and described? And who decides what is to be protected and how? These questions lie at the heart of a broader critique, one that moves beyond traditional state-centric paradigms to explore how security is socially and politically constituted. This study contributes to this reflection by adopting a discursive framework, which fundamentally challenges the core assumptions of conventional security studies. Conventional approaches typically presuppose that entities—mainly in the form of states—exist in an environment within which they face concrete, external threats. In this view, the nature of the entities in question is seen as fixed and given, and their "security is … understood to mean securing these fixed entities against objective and external threats" (Weldes et al., 1999, p. 9), often achieved through mechanisms of "spatial exclusion" (Dalby, 1992, p. 98).

The discursive perspective instead shifts the focus to the processes through which threats are constructed and rendered meaningful. Contemporary threats to the security of Europe illustrate that the very act of defining these phenomena as threats is inherently tied to broader political and institutional contexts and is carried out through discursive practices, based on the premise that "our access to reality is always through language" (Jørgensen & Phillips, 2002, p. 8). By scrutinising these processes, the discursive perspective provides valuable insights into how security is defined and practised within the European security landscape. This perspective not only highlights the contingent nature of security but also offers a lens to critically examine the interplay between discourse, power, and policy in shaping the so-called European security order. It assumes that while these threats may appear to target the fabric of societies, the well-being of individuals, and the values and principles underpinning democratic systems, their existence as threats depends on the meanings ascribed to them within the broader discourse. Contemporary threats—such as attacks on critical infrastructure, cyber intrusions, disinformation campaigns, and ideological extremism—are not simply pre-existing (or pre-discursive) phenomena waiting to be observed. Rather, they are actively constituted within specific political and institutional contexts. As Campbell argues, "[N]o one escapes the discursive realm of problematization to find themselves in an extra-discursive realm of pregiven problems and ready-made solutions. The latter always depends on the former" (1998a, pp. x–xi).

The processes of meaning-making take place through the security practices and discourses of actors, which render such phenomena intelligible as threats. The responses developed within the framework of security policy, in turn, "invest those enacting security policies with the legitimate *power* to undertake decisive and otherwise exceptional actions" while at the same time endowing "those actors with a particular *responsibility* for doing so" (L. Hansen, 2006, p. 35, emphasis original). This focus on those who take action underscores the centrality of discursive agents in security practices, as it is these actors—key decision-makers, state institutions, international organisations, or other security stakeholders—who interpret threats and rationalise the corresponding measures. By positioning themselves as both empowered to act and obligated to protect, these actors find their voice and reinforce their authority within the security framework. This dual process of empowerment and obligation highlights the deeply political nature of security. Far from being a neutral or fixed condition, security is a practice that not only defines what constitutes a threat but also determines the boundaries of appropriate and legitimate action, and, above all, who gets to decide and act.

While the theoretical dimension of rethinking security accentuates the constructed and political nature of threats, the substantive challenges facing European security reveal the expanding scope of what is considered 'security'. In this broader sense, security is no longer confined to the protection of borders or the preservation of state sovereignty. Instead, it extends to safeguarding the societal structures, fundamental rights, and shared norms that underpin democratic systems. This expansion reflects the increasingly multifaceted and interconnected features of contemporary threats, which often operate outside conventional military frameworks. Current threats—such as cyber intrusions, disinformation campaigns, foreign economic interference, and ideological extremism—are portrayed as posing risks not just to territorial integrity and sovereignty but also to societal cohesion and democratic institutions. Attacks on critical infrastructure, for instance, have the potential to disrupt essential services and erode public trust, while disinformation campaigns can undermine democratic processes by polarising communities and delegitimising institutions. Similarly, the rise of ideological extremism is deemed to threaten not only individual safety but also the values of pluralism and tolerance that are seen as central to European identity and way of life. Through this lens, the liberal democratic qualities of European states and societies are viewed "as vulnerabilities that can be exploited to drive wedges through democratic societies and undermine governability" (Wigell, 2019, p. 256). These non-conventional threats challenge habitual security responses, as they target vulnerabilities that are deeply embedded in the social, political, economic, and cultural fabric of communities and institutions.

Broadening the scope of security to include societal and political structures and values has resulted in the involvement of a wider range of actors. While states remain central, international organisations like NATO and the EU, alongside private entities and civil society, play increasingly prominent roles in addressing these multifaceted challenges. Their interpretations shape the responses deemed appropriate and legitimate—from public awareness campaigns and resilience-building to adaptation and active defence—highlighting the deeply contingent nature of how security challenges are understood and addressed.

Consequently, the rethinking of security, both theoretically and substantively, highlights the importance of viewing it as a contested and political practice. Security is not a predetermined condition but a fluid concept, devoid of a fixed definition, and a state that can never be fully achieved.

Multiple conceptions of security coexist, each shaped by differing political outlooks "that allow different perceptions of threat to emerge" (Bilgin, 2008, p. 91). The theoretical dimension reveals how threats and responses are constituted through social practices, emphasising the constructed nature of security/insecurity. Substantively, this rethinking broadens the scope of security beyond state sovereignty to include societal structures and shared values as objects of security. This dual lens aligns with post-structuralism's focus on the discursive processes of meaning-making, wherein actors—be it in the form of states, international organisations, or civil society—actively produce and reproduce the narratives, identities, and frameworks that define security and its associated practices.

Security Discourses and the Mapping of Space

Discourses are not mere linguistic acts; they involve "plays of power which mobilize rules, codes and procedures to assert a particular understanding, through the construction of knowledge within these rules, codes and procedures" (Dalby, 1988, p. 416). It is through the power inherent in discourses that positions and practices are defined and brought to life. In the realm of security, this means that what is identified as a threat, who is deemed responsible both as the object and as the subject of security, and what measures are considered appropriate are all shaped by the discursive construction of knowledge and meaning. Discourses do not merely reflect reality but actively shape it, creating the frameworks through which security actors interpret and respond to their environment. A comprehensive analysis of these discourses may "focus on their instantiations", yet their power resides "not on any particular instantiation but on their anonymous, unnoticed permeation of our ways of thinking and talking and making sense of the social world" (Brubaker & Cooper, 2000, p. 16).

A key attribute of the current security environment is its ambiguity, not only in terms of the sources and forms of threats but also in terms of how these threats are identified and framed. Contemporary threats are often depicted as pervasive and constantly evolving, with the methods employed to identify and counter them adapting correspondingly. As Rühle and Roberts note, "[t]he times when peace, crisis and conflict were three distinct phases, when conflicts were fought largely with military means, and when adversaries were well known, are over" (2021). States and societies today face threats that bypass conventional markers, "without a single soldier crossing a single border" (Rühle & Roberts, 2021). These changes complicate traditional understandings of security and space, and challenge the assumption that threats are clear-cut, objective, or external, revealing the need for a more comprehensive and adaptive approach to address challenges.

Yet, despite this ambiguity, the process of identifying an enemy—the Other against which the Self is to be protected—remains central to how security is understood and practised in Europe today. This delineation of the Self from the Other is not arbitrary but is actively created and maintained through processes of differentiation and exclusion. "The creation of social boundaries", continually produced, reproduced, and reinforced to define who or what constitutes a threat, is fundamental to this process (Neumann, 1999, p. 35). In the European context, the Self—the imagined collectivity of Europe as a political, social, and cultural space—is in constant need of aligning its various domains, which include its identity, territory, security, and governance. This alignment constantly requires its reproduction, which implies that Europe is "always in a process of becoming" (Campbell, 1998b, p. 12).

The theoretical position adopted in this study conceptualises security not as a pre-given or definitive state. Poststructuralist security studies emphasise that security is not about addressing objective threats in a straightforward manner but about constructing the boundaries of what constitutes a threat, who is responsible for addressing it, and what measures are deemed necessary. Discourses play a key role in this process because "they provide legitimacy, and indeed provide the intellectual conditions of possibility of particular institutional and political arrangements" (Dalby, 1988, p. 416). This includes the polities that are often treated as givens rather than outcomes of governance processes: "it is the meaning that actors attach to them that matters, not their formal characteristics" (A.D. Hansen & Sørensen, 2005, p. 95). Threats do not simply exist; they are interpreted, framed, and rendered intelligible within specific discourses, through specific narratives. These discourses shape not only policy structures and responses but also the broader political realities they claim to address, including discursive polities like the EU and the transatlantic security community encapsulated in NATO (Rogers, 2009). The ambiguity of the contemporary security environment creates a productive space for meaning-making, where those deemed responsible for the security of Europe actively define what is at risk and who must act to protect it. The constant framing of threats sustains and reinforces a specific reading of Europe as a cohesive entity under threat, requiring both protection and alignment across its domains.

In his analysis of NATO strategy during and after the Cold War, Klein observed that, despite the lack of empirical evidence concerning the scale of the "Soviet threat", persistent references to hypothetical questions like "what would happen if …?" reified a particular understanding of threats. This process established a series of conjectures about the nature of international politics, notably of a Hobbesian character (1990, p. 313). Klein concludes that, from the perspective of NATO strategists, the priority was "to construct certainty about life at home", with the external Soviet threat taking secondary importance (1990, p. 313). This observation is particularly striking, as it suggests that representations of external dangers were less about responding to immediate risks and more about mapping and maintaining the boundaries of the domestic and international order (Bilgin, 2008). In this respect, the practices that shaped NATO's creation and evolution were deeply political, not only concerned with security but also with constructing a specific reading of 'the West' within a mapped global space. Thus, institutions like NATO not only symbolised "a pre-existing Western security community united around liberal-democratic norms and values" but also actively constructed a particular understanding of 'the West' (Gheciu, 2019, p. 33). Klein, in fact, argues that "NATO as a political practice constructed a particular architecture of global space" (1990, p. 314)—an architecture defined by sharp divisions between 'us' and 'them'. These divisions were spatial as well as ideological, and NATO's practices played a crucial role in delineating zones of safety and danger. The spatial logic of NATO's policies was institutionalised through key organisations, such as the International Institute for Strategic Studies, which, as Klein notes, "became a site for the articulation of a Western strategic consensus, not necessarily in terms of complete agreement, but in terms of the *language* and *policy problems* that came widely to be shared among responsible managers of alliance affairs" (1990, p. 317, emphasis added).

This spatial dimension of NATO's practices reveals that its success in deterring the Soviet threat and avoiding actual war was "the only feasible means of securing that precarious construct called 'the Western way of life'" (Klein, 1990, p. 319). This was mapped onto global space through continual border-drawing exercises—political, ideological, and territorial—that distinguished 'the West' from the rest. These practices not only defined zones of influence and control but also reinforced the West as a singular, coherent identity existing beyond politics. For Europe, this mapping of space extended beyond traditional notions of defence to encompass the maintenance of ontological security (Mitzen, 2006; Steele, 2008). By continually reasserting these boundaries, NATO sustained a shared sense of identity and purpose for Europe within the imagined space of the West.

Through this lens, it can be deduced that the current policies of both the EU and NATO are not tailor-made reactions developed "as a response to a threatening reality 'out there' that offered no alternative" (George, 1994, p. 3). Instead, these policies emerge through specific discourses, containing narratives that actively shape how challenges and threats to European security are perceived and addressed. By framing certain issues as threats, the EU and NATO effectively map a discursive space where certain actions and responses are legitimised while others are excluded. Their discursive practices do not reflect a pre-existing security reality; they actively construct it, embedding particular understandings of Europe's vulnerabilities, enemies, and the means necessary to protect its integrity. This suggests that alternative interpretations of the world are also possible, underscoring the existence of "many and varied sites of activity, men and women make their worlds and retain the potential to change them" (George, 1994, p. 3).

Narratives, Leitmotifs, and Hybrid Threats

"Humans are, among other things, story-telling beings", argues Devetak (2009, p. 795). Narratives are inherent to our everyday lives, serving not only as tools for organising our experiences but also as the stories through which we make sense of them. Through narratives, we simplify "complex situations into chains of events" and comprehend them as parts of a sequence—temporally and relationally (Shenhav, 2006, p. 246). These narratives shape our understandings, actions, and identities, influencing not only individuals but also the Self in relation to the Other at the international level (Spencer, 2016).

In the field of IR, the study of narratives has become part of what some call the 'narrative turn' in social research (Czarniawska, 2004; Roberts, 2006) and the 'linguistic turn' in international studies.[1] While often used interchangeably with terms like discourse, rhetoric, or argumentation, the

[1] For a critical account of IR's turns, see Baele and Bettiza (2021).

concept of 'narrative' has its roots in narratology—the study of how stories are structured and how they shape our perceptions of reality. Adapted largely from literary studies and history, the narrative approach reframes accounts of international politics, treating them as "more or less convincing stories" rather than objective depictions of universal truths or "law-like regularities" (Kuusisto, 2020, p. 4) in IR. In this view, what IR scholars present is merely one specific interpretation or narrative of international politics independent of their choice not to narrativise it through "nonnarrative, even antinarrative modes of representation" (White, 1987, p. 2). The analysis of these narratives, in turn, explores how actors exist and "act through the stories they tell about themselves" and others (Subotić, 2016, p. 614). These mainly autobiographical narratives situate actors temporally and spatially within a web of relationships, defining their position in the international system. By highlighting that any narrative is one among many alternatives, narrative analysis has the potential to reveal "how certain understandings of the world become and remain dominant while others fail to gain traction" (Spencer, 2016, p. 13).

There are different ways of approaching narratives, which mainly revolve around questions of agency and intentionality. Narratives can be seen as stories that are tailor-made and strategically utilised by the political elite to influence public opinion and the behaviour of domestic or international actors in their efforts "to extend their influence, manage expectations, and change the discursive environment in which they operate" (Miskimmon et al., 2013, p. 3). Such an instrumental view highlights the purposeful construction and employment of narratives by 'narrative entrepreneurs' who selectively create, represent, and promote them (Crank et al., 2008; Subotić, 2016). Another option is to approach narratives as a higher structure of meaning, possessing power independent of these political elites. Through this lens, narratives constrain what can be meaningfully said or done by the audience and the decision-makers, as they are all "inextricably bound up with discourses that leave them little room for individuality" (Spencer, 2016, p. 4). Studies that operate on this assumption are focused more on political narratives themselves as well as "what narratives do in politics" within the broader framework provided by specific discourses (Oppermann & Spencer, 2023, p. 119). This study adopts the latter view, examining narratives as structures of meaning that shape and constrain both individual and collective agency. By treating narratives as frameworks embedded within broader discursive structures, this analysis seeks to uncover how they influence political realities and shape the conditions of possibility in the realm of security.

In the preface to his seminal *The Content of the Form*, White asserts that "narrative is not merely a discursive form that may or may not be used to represent real events in their aspect as developmental processes but rather entails ontological and epistemic choices with distinct ideological and even specifically political implications" (1987, p. ix). This observation has significant repercussions for international politics and security. Narratives, as White suggests, are not neutral representations of reality but frameworks that embed specific ontological and epistemic choices. They do not directly or causally determine actions or policies; instead, they shape the conditions under which actions become conceivable. As Subotić explains, narratives enable and constrain action, "making action possible, allowing for some practices and policies, while foreclosing possibility for others" (2016, p. 613). Thus, narratives exert a subtle yet profound influence, shaping how social reality is constructed.

Discourse and narratives are deeply interconnected, with narratives functioning as the building blocks that structure and give coherence to broader discourses (Oppermann & Spencer, 2023). Such a view departs from conventional poststructuralist accounts by highlighting the active role of narratives in shaping and structuring meaning within different contexts. Narratives provide the stories through which discourses are articulated, shaping how events, identities, and relationships are understood and represented (Somers, 1994). A single discourse can encompass multiple narratives, which may align with, complement, or contradict one other, reflecting the contested and dynamic nature of meaning-making processes. In this way, narratives structure overarching discourses while leaving room for alternative or counter-narratives. Narrative analysis is a method of discourse analysis that seeks to uncover these very structures (Spencer, 2016).

Narratives are typically stories that unfold in a sequential order, characterised by "a clear beginning, middle and end" (Hinchman & Hinchman, 1997, p. xv). However, these stories are not mere chronological records of events; they consist of interconnected parts that together form a meaningful whole. As Hinchman and Hinchman explain, narratives "add up" because "the units so ordered must have an intrinsic, meaningful connection to one another" (1997, p. xv). This intrinsic connection transforms a series of events into a coherent and purposeful story. This coherence is achieved through the plot, which integrates events into a unified structure

(Bremond, 1980). The plot provides not only chronological order but also causal relationships that give meaning to the sequence of events. By organising events around themes, objectives, or, in the current case, a leitmotif, narratives transform uncoordinated occurrences into meaningful events. In this respect, narratives serve as a powerful tool for making sense of complex realities.

The term 'leitmotif' originally refers to "a recurrent musical idea which has been invested by its composer with semantic content", as Warren Darcy explains (Darcy, 1993, p. 45). An anglicised version of the German term *leitmotiv* (leading motif), the concept of leitmotif is often associated with Richard Wagner's *Der Ring des Nibelungen* as well as the more current works of Richard Strauss and Arnold Schönberg, particularly the epic *Gurre-Lieder*. In music, leitmotif is a structural motif tied to specific characters, situations, or emotions, unifying and deepening the narrative through repetition and variation. Leitmotifs continuously evolve and carry with them an emotional association; as such they simultaneously "contribute to and function within a larger musical structure" (Bribitzer-Stull, 2015, p. 10).

While its origins are in music, the concept of the leitmotif has transcended its original context and can also be used to denote a recurring theme, image, or idea often imbued with special meaning within a discourse or narrative. In this broader sense, the leitmotif functions as a structural thread that ties together disparate elements, reinforcing a central theme or organising principle. In political discourse, a leitmotif might take the form of a recurring metaphor, slogan, or symbol that evokes particular associations and shapes public perception. The power of a leitmotif lies in its ability to accumulate layers of meaning through repetition and context. Each recurrence reaffirms its symbolic significance while subtle variations adapt it to new circumstances, allowing it to evolve alongside the narrative. As such, the leitmotif serves not only as an organising element but also as a tool for encoding political or cultural resonance, making it a particularly potent mechanism in shaping narratives and framing understanding.

In the context of European security, hybrid threats take on the function of a leitmotif, recurring across policy discussions, strategic frameworks, and political discourse. Hybrid threats, with their multifaceted and ambiguous nature, serve as a symbolic and unifying thread in European security narratives, providing coherence to diverse security concerns while reflecting the dynamic and evolving nature of contemporary threats. The power of hybrid threats as a leitmotif lies in their symbolic potency, adaptability, and vagueness. Each recurrence of the term reinforces its salience, framing it as the ultimate embodiment of uncertainty, risk, and complexity in the security landscape. Through repetition in political statements, policy documents, and reports, hybrid threats gain an almost mythic quality, signifying the persistent and pervasive vulnerabilities faced by Europe. At the same time, subtle variations in its usage adapt the leitmotif to different contexts, whether addressing cyber warfare, electoral interference, or energy dependency. This flexibility allows the leitmotif of hybrid threats to stay relevant while shaping and constraining the discourse surrounding European security.

By positioning hybrid threats as the leitmotif in European security narratives, this study examines how this theme shapes the conditions of possibility for action. It argues that much like a leitmotif in a musical composition, hybrid threats unify disparate elements—geopolitical tensions, infrastructural vulnerabilities, and ideological conflicts—into a cohesive framework. This not only structures the discourse but also imbues a continued sense of insecurity, evolving dangers, and risks, which reinforces a shared feeling of imminent danger and the need for collective action at different levels within Europe.

Narrative Components and Their Analysis: How the Story Unfolds

Narratives are distinguished from other forms of communication by their identifiable components and structured flow (Kohler Riessman, 2008, p. 5). As part of broader discourses, narratives typically follow a sequential structure that organises events into a coherent story that starts with the possibility of action, follows the pursuit of it, and concludes with its outcomes: virtuality, actualisation, and realisation, in short (Bertens, 2014, p. 128). These three phases, though at times overlapping and interwoven in different sequences, structure narratives and shape the way in which any story is told in a chronological manner. By examining the sequential arrangement of events, the roles of actors, and the moral or ideological lessons conveyed, narrative analysis reveals the underlying assumptions driving a given narrative.

While narrative analysis is a form of discourse analysis, it provides distinct methodological tools by focusing on the specific structures and elements of storytelling. One of the key strengths of narrative analysis lies in its structured approach, rooted in identifiable components. These components serve as analytical anchors, offering researchers a systematic framework to examine how meaning is constructed, communicated, and sustained over time. This enables a more systematic breakdown of narratives compared to broader discourse analysis, which accentuates the fluidity of meaning-making (L. Hansen, 2006). The role attributed to the narrator, which all but disappears within the story, is of particular importance as it underscores the urge to narrate—to make sense of seemingly disparate happenings (White, 1981, p. 3). It is through the lenses of these narrators that the story is told, a practice that reinforces the positions of certain actors "while disempowering others depending on their discursive strategies", which ultimately affects the "distribution of political power" and determines who gets to speak on behalf of what (Homolar, 2011, pp. 706–707).

Narrative analysis enhances the researcher's toolkit, facilitating a deeper understanding of how stories resonate with audiences and shape representations of events, identities, and actions. Moreover, it is particularly effective in uncovering recurring patterns, themes, and power dynamics embedded within storytelling. This makes narrative analysis especially relevant in the study of security, where framing issues as threats often relies on compelling and persuasive narratives. As a method, it enables researchers to trace how threats are constructed, responses justified, and policies aligned with or challenged by broader political discourses.

Narratives are typically built around three key components. They occur within specific *settings* and feature a number of *characters* that enact particular storylines through *emplotment*—the process of organising events into a coherent story (Oppermann & Spencer, 2023, p. 120; Devetak, 2009). Emplotment acts as the connective tissue, weaving together the setting, envisaged as "the stage set of a theatre play providing the context in which narrative unfolds" (Oppermann & Spencer, 2023, p. 120), and the characters that drive the story in a meaningful direction. By linking these elements through temporal sequences (the order of events) and causal relationships (connections between actions and their consequences) (Spencer, 2016; Shenhav, 2006), emplotment transforms independent events into a cohesive story which serves as "the intelligible whole that governs a succession of events in any story" (Ricoeur, 1981, p. 167) (Fig. 2.1).

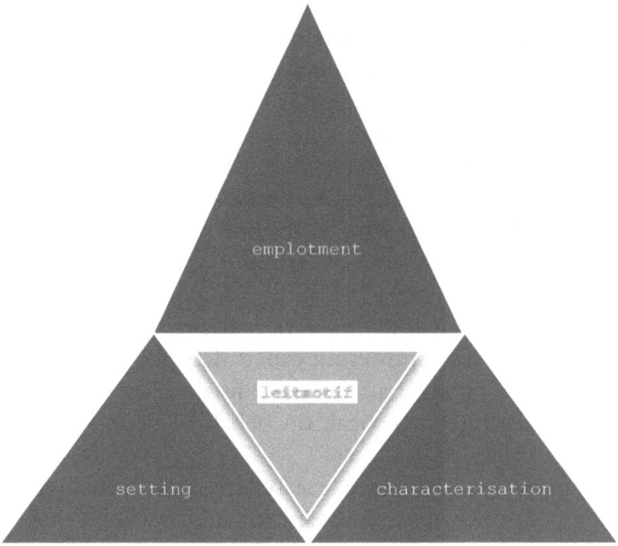

Fig. 2.1 Narrative structure and the role of the leitmotif

Policy narratives are stories that "underwrite and stabilize the assumptions for policymaking in situations that persist with many unknowns, a high degree of interdependence, and little, if any, agreement" (Roe, 1994, p. 34). These narratives not only provide a meaningful framework for interpreting the current situation but also guide the selection of appropriate actions to achieve specific objectives. By doing so, policy narratives articulate a particular understanding of identity, shaping how actors perceive themselves and their position within the international system.

In the context of European security, narrative components provide a useful lens to examine how NATO and the EU construct themselves and their responses. Setting defines the European security landscape as fraught with diffuse, evolving threats; characters are the key protagonists—NATO and the EU—and their adversaries; and emplotment ties these elements into coherent storylines that justify their actions.

Through their narratives, NATO and the EU articulate their distinct yet complementary positions within the European security architecture. The division of labour between them is not merely practical; it is also discursively constructed, reinforcing their complementary roles. By aligning their roles within the European security architecture, NATO and the EU project an image of seamless collaboration. Through these narratives, they legitimise their actions and establish what is at stake in terms of Europe's security and their respective roles and responsibilities. NATO often leads on military deterrence, invoking its historic role as the defender of the collective 'West'. This role is rooted in a long-standing spatial and ideological division between East and West, reinforced by NATO's portrayal of threats such as a resurgent Russia and destabilising hybrid tactics. This framing is not new but builds on NATO's origins as a protector of "Western civilisation", a concept with deep historical roots (Jackson, 2003, p. 240). The setting of NATO's narrative is often framed as one of ideological and spatial tension, with the West representing democratic values and the East symbolising authoritarian threats. Its characters include both the collective West (with NATO as its defender) and adversaries like Russia and China, which embody disruptive forces in this dichotomy.

In contrast, the EU positions itself as a stabilising force, integrating societal, economic, and infrastructural dimensions into its security narrative. By prioritising resilience—framed as the capacity to absorb and adapt to shocks—the EU legitimises its identity as a guardian of unity and European values. This narrative aligns with its "top-down project" to position itself as the central actor in Europe's security and defence policy, often at the expense of alternative frameworks (Rogers, 2009, p. 834). The EU's characteristic traits portray it as a unifying and integrative force, with its member states as beneficiaries of its protective policies. Its emplotment weaves these elements into a story of resilience and adaptability, presenting the EU as essential for overcoming diverse and diffuse threats.

It must be remembered that these narratives are neither neutral nor uncontested. They are constructed and contingent, reflecting political decisions about how to frame threats and responses. For example, the dominant focus on military deterrence and resilience marginalises alternative approaches, such as those emphasising diplomacy, systemic reform, or de-escalation. In narrative terms, these alternatives represent excluded or marginalised storylines, overshadowed by the dominant framing of NATO and the EU as indispensable protectors of European stability. By interrogating the constructed nature of NATO and the EU's security narratives, it becomes possible to uncover their political underpinnings and open up space for reconsidering Europe's security outlook. This perspective challenges the assumption of a singular, objective understanding of security, instead highlighting the potential for alternative interpretations. In doing so, it underscores the importance of critically examining how the elements of setting, characterisation, and emplotment interact to shape security discourse, influencing not only policy decisions but also perceptions of what is possible in the realm of European security.

The analysis focuses on texts emanating from NATO and the EU, their affiliated bodies, as well as statements and contributions from key representatives since the term ‘hybrid threats’ entered their political agendas. These representatives include NATO Secretaries General, EU High Representatives for Foreign Affairs and Security Policy, and other senior officials involved in security and defence. The primary sources for this analysis include official declarations, policy papers, strategy documents, and public speeches. These texts provide a comprehensive basis for understanding how hybrid threats have been constructed, communicated, and operationalised over time (Table 2.1).

The narrative framework employs the three components discussed earlier—setting, characterisation, and emplotment—to examine and interpret these materials. The setting refers to the European security environment as envisaged by NATO and the EU, encompassing the geopolitical, institutional, and societal contexts within which hybrid threats are framed and addressed. The characters include NATO and the EU as principal actors, along with their sub-units and affiliated institutions, a key one being the European Centre of Excellence for Countering Hybrid Threats (Hybrid CoE) in Helsinki. The emplotment involves analysing the stories these organisations construct about the evolution of hybrid threats, focusing on

Table 2.1 The coding of narratives

Setting	*Characterisation*	*Emplotment*
The backdrop Where and against which backdrop do the events take place? How does this backdrop shape the characters and their responses? In what ways does the setting impact on how the story unfolds?	*Main characters and their identities* How are the characters labelled and described? What sorts of behaviour are expected from the characters? What are their dispositions? How do these characters engage with the other actors in the story?	*The story* What is the overarching story that brings the setting and characters together in a meaningful way? How is the story temporally, spatially, and relationally narrated? What are the key turning points in the story and how frequently do they occur?

Adapted from Oppermann and Spencer (2023), Spencer (2016)

how the emergence, development, and implications of these challenges are narrated. These components collectively demonstrate how hybrid threats, as a leitmotif, serve to unify disparate elements of the discourse while reinforcing the centrality of NATO and the EU in addressing them.

This narrative-based approach reveals the recurring themes and underlying assumptions embedded in NATO and EU discourses about hybrid threats. By examining how the setting is framed, how the characters are positioned, and how the plotlines are constructed, the analysis uncovers the broader political and discursive strategies shaping European security. Hybrid threats, as the leitmotif of these narratives, not only provide coherence but also serve as a mechanism for legitimising specific policy decisions and institutional roles. This analysis thus highlights how the concept of hybrid threats has evolved to become a central organising theme in the construction of Europe's security order, shaping both its present and its future.

Bibliography

Baele, S. J., & Bettiza, G. (2021). 'Turning' Everywhere in IR: On the Sociological Underpinnings of the Field's Proliferating Turns. *International Theory, 13*(2), 314–340. https://doi.org/10.1017/S1752971920000172

Bertens, H. (2014). *Literary Theory: The Basics* (3rd ed.). Routledge.

Bilgin, P. (2008). Critical Theory. In P. D. Williams (Ed.), *Security Studies: An Introduction* (pp. 89–102). Routledge.

Bremond, C. (1980). The Logic of Narrative Possibilities (E. D. Cancalon, Trans.). *New Literary History, 11*(3), 387–411. https://doi.org/10.2307/468934

Bribitzer-Stull, M. (2015). *Understanding the Leitmotif: From Wagner to Hollywood Film Music.* Cambridge University Press.

Brubaker, R., & Cooper, F. (2000). Beyond 'Identity'. *Theory and Society, 29*(1), 1–47.

Campbell, D. (1998a). *National Deconstruction: Violence, Identity, and Justice in Bosnia.* University of Minnesota Press.

Campbell, D. (1998b). *Writing Security: United States Foreign Policy and the Politics of Identity.* University of Minnesota Press.

Crank, J. P., Hoffman, D., & Conn, M. (2008). The 'War on Terror' and Iraq: The Collapse of a Hegemonic Narrative. *Homeland Security Review, 2*(1), 29–56.

Czarniawska, B. (Ed.). (2004). *Narratives in Social Science Research.* Sage.

Dalby, S. (1988). Geopolitical Discourse: The Soviet Union as Other. *Alternatives, 13*(4), 415–442.

Dalby, S. (1992). Security, Modernity, Ecology: The Dilemmas of Post-Cold War Security Discourse. *Alternatives, 17*(1), 95–134. https://doi.org/10.1177/030437549201700104

Darcy, W. (1993). *Wagner's Das Rheingold*. Oxford University Press.

Devetak, R. (2009). After the event: Don DeLillo's White Noise and September 11 Narratives. *Review of International Studies, 35*(4), 795–815. https://doi.org/10.1017/S0260210509990192

George, J. (1994). *Discourses of Global Politics: A Critical (Re)Introduction to International Relations*. Lynne Rienner.

Gheciu, A. (2019). NATO, Liberal Internationalism, and the Politics of Imagining the Western Security Community. *International Journal, 74*(1), 32–46. https://doi.org/10.1177/0020702019834645

Hansen, A. D., & Sørensen, E. (2005). Polity as Politics: Studying the Shaping and Effects of Discursive Polities. In D. Howarth & J. Torfing (Eds.), *Discourse Theory in European Politics: Identity, Policy and Governance* (pp. 93–116). Palgrave Macmillan. https://doi.org/10.1057/9780230523364

Hansen, L. (2006). *Security as Practice: Discourse Analysis and the Bosnian War*. Routledge.

Hinchman, L. P., & Hinchman, S. K. (1997). Introduction. In L. P. Hinchman & S. K. Hinchman (Eds.), *Memory, Identity, Community: The Idea of Narrative in the Human Sciences* (pp. xiii–xxxii). State University of New York Press.

Homolar, A. (2011). Rebels Without a Conscience: The Evolution of the Rogue States Narrative in US Security Policy. *European Journal of International Relations, 17*(4), 705–727. https://doi.org/10.1177/1354066110383996

Jackson, P. T. (2003). Defending the West: Occidentalism and the Formation of NATO. *The Journal of Political Philosophy, 11*(3), 223–252.

Jørgensen, M., & Phillips, L. (2002). *Discourse Analysis as Theory and Method*. SAGE.

Klein, B. S. (1990). How the West was One: Representational Politics of NATO. *International Studies Quarterly, 34*(3), 311–325. https://doi.org/10.2307/2600572

Kohler Riessman, C. (2008). *Narrative Methods for the Human Sciences*. Sage.

Kuusisto, R. (2020). *International Relations Narratives: Plotting World Politics*. Routledge.

Miskimmon, A., O'Loughlin, B., & Roselle, L. (2013). *Strategic Narratives: Communication Power and the New World Order*. Routledge. https://doi.org/10.4324/9781315871264

Mitzen, J. (2006). Ontological Security in World Politics: State Identity and the Security Dilemma. *European Journal of International Relations, 12*(3), 341–370. https://doi.org/10.1177/1354066106067346

Neumann, I. B. (1999). *Uses of the other: 'The East' in European identity formation.* Manchester University Press.

Oppermann, K., & Spencer, A. (2023). Narrative Analysis. In P. A. Mello & F. Ostermann (Eds.), *Routledge Handbook of Foreign Policy Analysis Methods* (pp. 117–132). Routledge. https://doi.org/10.4324/9781003139850-11

Ricoeur, P. (1981). Narrative Time. In W. J. T. Mitchell (Ed.), *On Narrative* (pp. 165–186). University of Chicago Press.

Roberts, G. (2006). History, Theory and the Narrative Turn in IR. *Review of International Studies, 32*(4), 703–714. https://doi.org/10.1017/S0260210506007248

Roe, E. (1994). *Narrative Policy Analysis: Theory and Practice.* Duke University Press.

Rogers, J. (2009). From 'Civilian Power' to 'Global Power': Explicating the European Union's 'Grand Strategy' Through the Articulation of Discourse Theory. *JCMS. Journal of Common Market Studies, 47*(4), 831–862.

Rühle, M., & Roberts, C. (2021). Enlarging NATO's Toolbox to Counter Hybrid Threats. *NATO Review.* https://www.nato.int/docu/review/articles/2021/03/19/enlarging-natos-toolbox-to-counter-hybrid-threats/index.html

Shenhav, S. R. (2006). Political Narratives and Political Reality. *International Political Science Review, 27*(3), 245–262.

Somers, M. R. (1994). The Narrative Constitution of Identity: A Relational and Network Approach. *Theory and Society, 23*(5), 605–649.

Spencer, A. (2016). *Romantic Narratives in international Politics: Pirates, Rebels and Mercenaries.* Manchester University Press.

Steele, B. J. (2008). *Ontological Security in International Relations: Self-Identity and the IR State.* Routledge.

Subotić, J. (2016). Narrative, Ontological Security, and Foreign Policy Change. *Foreign Policy Analysis, 12*(4), 610–627. https://doi.org/10.1111/fpa.12089

Weldes, J., Laffey, M., Gusterson, H., & Duvall, R. (1999). Introduction: Constructing Insecurity. In J. Weldes, M. Laffey, H. Gusterson, & R. Duvall (Eds.), *Cultures of Insecurity: States, Communities, and the Production of Danger* (pp. 1–33). University of Minnesota Press.

White, H. (1981). The Value of Narrativity in the Representation of Reality. In W. J. T. Mitchell (Ed.), *On Narrative* (pp. 1–23). University of Chicago Press.

White, H. (1987). *The Content of the Form: Narrative Discourse and Historical Representation.* Johns Hopkins University Press.

Wigell, M. (2019). Hybrid Interference as a Wedge Strategy: A Theory of External Interference in Liberal Democracy. *International Affairs, 95*(2), 255–275. https://doi.org/10.1093/ia/iiz018

CHAPTER 3

Narratives on European Security and the Leitmotif of Hybrid Threats

Russia, China, but also North Korea and Iran, are hard
at work to try to weaken North America and Europe.
To chip away at our freedom.
They want to reshape the global order.
Not to create a fairer one, but to secure their own spheres of influence.
They are testing us.
And the rest of the world is watching.
No, we are not at war.
But we are certainly not at peace either.
NATO Secretary General Mark Rutte, Brussels, 12 December 2024

"A spectre is haunting the Western world", Mälksoo notes (2018, p. 374), the spectre of all things hybrid in security. The prevalent use of the term 'hybrid' has become a defining feature of current narratives emanating from European security institutions, most notably NATO and the EU. Terms such as 'hybrid war/warfare', 'hybrid threats', 'hybrid strategies', 'hybrid tactics', and 'hybrid activities' pervade strategic documents, public statements, and policy discussions, underscoring the centrality of the notion of hybridity in the European security lexicon. The focus on hybridity reflects a fundamental shift in security thinking, where the boundaries between war and peace become increasingly blurred. This poses a significant challenge in terms of the legal grey zone it creates,

Z. Arkan, *European Security and Hybrid Threats*,
https://doi.org/10.1007/978-3-031-86793-4_3

which affects "the application of the rules governing the use of force, including the exercise of the right of individual and collective self-defense" (Sari, 2019, p. 442). It is within this context that the notion of hybrid threats emerges, encapsulating the fluid and multifaceted nature of contemporary security challenges. Coupled with the wide spectrum of potential threats it encompasses—from investment and migration to technology and research—the prevalence of hybrid threats ultimately paves the way for the securitisation and "weaponisation of everything" (Galeotti, 2022).

A basic definition by NATO underscores the open-endedness of the notion: "Hybrid threats combine military and non-military as well as covert and overt means, including disinformation, cyber attacks, economic pressure, deployment of irregular armed groups and use of regular forces. Hybrid methods are used to blur the lines between war and peace, and attempt to sow doubt in the minds of target populations. They aim to destabilise and undermine societies" (NATO, 2024b).

The EU's definition of the term adopts a similarly broad and ambiguous tone: "Hybrid threats combine conventional and unconventional, military and non-military activities that can be used in a coordinated manner by state or non-state actors to achieve specific political objectives. Hybrid campaigns are multidimensional, combining coercive and subversive measures, using both conventional and unconventional tools and tactics. They are designed to be difficult to detect or attribute. These threats target critical vulnerabilities and seek to create confusion to hinder swift and effective decision-making" (European External Action Service—EEAS, 2018). To render this definition more concrete, the EU provides illustrative examples: "Hybrid threats can range from cyberattacks on critical information systems, through the disruption of critical services such as energy supplies or financial services, to the undermining of public trust in government institutions or the deepening of social divisions" (EEAS, 2018). As these definitions suggest, the open-endedness of hybrid threats extends beyond the subjects, objects, and domains of security to include the means and methods employed, further embedding hybridity as a central yet indeterminate theme in current security narratives.

The widespread use of the term 'hybrid' within security narratives carries profound implications. Rather than providing clarity and precision, it fosters a pervasive sense of fluidity, indeterminacy, and ambiguity. This places policymakers in a difficult position, compelling them to anticipate potential dangers and design policy responses in an environment defined by uncertainty. Framing insecurities as potential risks across multiple levels, security policies increasingly shift towards a proactive and anticipatory form of governance, seeking to foresee and plan "ahead of emergencies" in an uncertain environment (Umbach, 2024, p. 410). This transformation frames security as a domain focused on identifying, mitigating, and adapting to perceived risks, rather than addressing their structural or political roots.[1] Consequently, security becomes less about eliminating threats and more about managing the uncertainties they produce. Such transformation generates anxiety, driven by "the construction of threats so opaque and widespread that they cannot be readily resolved", which leads to the adoption of "a range of pre-emptive security measures across all possible areas of social life" (Eberle & Daniel, 2022, p. 4). This evolution underscores how the narrative of hybrid threats not only reflects but actively shapes the contours of contemporary security practices, embedding risk management, anticipation, and foresight into the very fabric of governance.

The Hybrid Threat Leitmotif: An Evolution

The notion of hybrid threats has become a cornerstone of European security discourse, encapsulating the ambiguities and complexities of modern conflict. This notion did not, however, originate within European institutions but evolved from American military discourse in the early 2000s. Scholars like Hoffman were pivotal in developing the term, defining it as the integration of "a full range of different modes of warfare including conventional capabilities, irregular tactics and formations, terrorist acts including indiscriminate violence and coercion, and criminal disorder" (Hoffman, 2007, p. 8). Hoffman's work was rooted in the American military's reflections on asymmetric warfare, highlighting how adversaries could combine state and non-state actors, cyber capabilities, and disinformation to exploit systemic vulnerabilities. The concept gained traction during the wars in Iraq and Afghanistan, where irregular and traditional military tactics increasingly blurred the lines between categories of conflict.

While initially an American military concept, the idea of hybrid threats was rapidly adapted and reframed in the European context, particularly after Russia's annexation of Crimea in 2014, which is often described as a turning point in European thinking. Russia's deployment of 'little green

[1] For a stimulating analysis of post-Cold War security and NATO from the perspective of the literature on risk society, see M. J. Williams (2009).

men'—unmarked military personnel—alongside disinformation campaigns, cyberattacks, and economic coercion demonstrated the effectiveness of hybrid tactics in achieving strategic objectives while remaining below the threshold of conventional warfare. The watershed event was interpreted as a stern warning by NATO and the EU, revealing how hybrid threats could destabilise democratic societies and undermine collective security frameworks without triggering traditional mechanisms of defence.

From this point on, NATO and the EU began crafting hybrid threats into a compelling narrative that would underpin their security outlooks. NATO's Wales Summit (NATO, 2014a) was the first institutional response that acknowledged hybrid warfare as a core security challenge, urging resilience and collective defence to counter the nebulous and adaptive nature of current threats. The Warsaw Summit (NATO, 2016b) further formalised this narrative, integrating hybrid threats into NATO's deterrence strategies, emphasising resilience, collective defence, and collaboration with the EU. Similarly, the EU's Global Strategy (EUGS) (EEAS, 2016) framed hybrid threats as emblematic of the contested international order, linking them to broader existential risks facing democratic societies and the rules-based global system. These practices naturalised hybrid threats as integral to the security landscape, utilising "seemingly 'objective' vocabularies and diagnostic terms" to present these threats as self-evident categories (Bertens, 2014, p. 124). This process not only reproduced a persistent sense of insecurity but also structured perceptions of global realities and influenced corresponding security responses. This dynamic reflects what Bertens (2014, p. 131) describes as an indirect form of power, where narratives create and sustain the conditions for their own reproduction.

In this context, NATO and the EU emerged as the key narrators of hybrid threats, crafting strategic stories that integrated their complementary roles as indispensable guardians of security and democracy in Europe. Through their policy documents, declarations, and strategic initiatives, these institutions embedded hybrid threats into the fabric of European security discourse. By defining the threats, characterising the actors, and weaving together a coherent story of collective defence and resilience, NATO and the EU have transformed hybridity into a cornerstone of transatlantic cooperation.

The establishment of the Hybrid CoE in 2017 as a joint effort by NATO and the EU further institutionalised this narrative, offering a dedicated platform for research, training, and strategy development. Documents drafted and published by Hybrid CoE reify and cultivate this particular conceptualisation of hybrid threats, framing them as multidimensional, adaptive, and inherently ambiguous, capable of targeting vulnerabilities across political, social, and technological domains. The Centre plays a pivotal role in formalising the narrative of hybrid threats, influencing how NATO and the EU frame their roles as defenders of democratic values and the rules-based order. More than just an institution, the Hybrid CoE also functions as a storyteller of European security, shaping how hybrid threats are framed and integrated into policy narratives. By framing hybrid threats as omnipresent and existential, the Centre constructs a security landscape (setting) where the boundaries between peace and conflict are deliberately blurred, and democratic institutions are under constant pressure.

The Hybrid CoE is equally instrumental in shaping the characterisation of the actors within this narrative. NATO and the EU are portrayed as steadfast defenders of democracy, working collaboratively to protect societies against adversaries—typically authoritarian regimes like Russia or China—that thrive on ambiguity and disruption. This dual narrative legitimises the EU and NATO's roles while painting adversaries as existential threats to the rules-based order. The Centre weaves these elements into a coherent storyline (emplotment) that situates NATO and the EU as central actors in an ongoing battle for resilience and survival. Through vivid depictions of high-profile cyberattacks and disinformation campaigns, it creates an urgent narrative that underscores the need for collective defence, foresight, and proactive countermeasures.

This evolution in security narratives, where hybrid threats are framed as pervasive and ambiguous risks, coincides with the increasing prominence of 'resilience' as a guiding notion in policy responses. Resilience emerged in European security discourse as both a reaction to and a framework for addressing the inherent unpredictability, uncertainty, and interconnectedness of contemporary challenges (Joseph & Juncos, 2024). NATO and the EU began to integrate resilience into their strategies as an all-encompassing response, with resilience often presented as an inherent attribute of democratic societies and institutions. This framing aligned closely with the anticipatory governance perspective, focusing on adaptability, preparation, and the capacity to absorb shocks rather than resolving the structural sources of insecurity.

As Joseph and Juncos argue, "[t]he discourse of resilience seeks governance through complexity and uncertainty, placing emphasis on the contingent, unstable and unknowable character of reality" (2019, p. 997). Since current threats are characterised by their fluidity and ability to exploit vulnerabilities across social, political, and economic domains, resilience serves as a useful means to reinforce systems and societies against these dispersed and unforeseeable risks. Critics emphasise how resilience is embedded in risk management frameworks, further entrenching a shift away from addressing systemic vulnerabilities towards continuous risk adaptation. Chandler (2014) describes resilience as 'the governance of complexity', one that eschews definitive solutions in favour of promoting flexibility and responsiveness. In a similar vein, Duffield (2016) critiques the resilience paradigm for treating insecurity as a perpetual condition to be managed rather than resolved, effectively resigning governance to a mode of constant adaptation. Joseph argues that by "constructing a picture of a world that is beyond our control" (2013, p. 42), the discourse on resilience embeds a depoliticised and technocratic logic into security practices by "emphasising individual responsibility, adaptability and preparedness" (2013, p. 40).

Resilience thus mirrors the vagueness of the hybrid threat narrative: just as hybrid threats are defined by their ambiguity, resilience is characterised by its broad, often unquantifiable pledge to prepare societies for risks that cannot be fully anticipated or understood. This alignment allows resilience to function as a complementary narrative device, reinforcing the hybrid threat framework while offering little in the way of tangible, structural solutions. Resilience does not seek to eliminate hybrid threats or address their root causes but instead normalises insecurity as a permanent condition, shifting the burden of security from institutions to individuals and communities (Joseph, 2013).

Within these evolving narratives on European security, hybridity becomes central to how threats are conceptualised and addressed. Using this diagnostic framework, the following part elucidates how hybrid threats structure European security by shaping the setting (context), the respective identities, roles, and responsibilities of NATO and the EU (characterisation), and the threat perceptions, actions, and policy responses adopted within this context (emplotment).

NATO Narratives on European Security Through the Leitmotif of Hybrid Threats

Early Days: Wales Summit Declaration (2014) and Warsaw Summit Communiqué (2016)

Setting: The Return of Civilisational Divisions

NATO's engagement with hybrid threats began amidst a resurgence of civilisational divides, epitomised by Russia's annexation of Crimea in 2014. This event marked a turning point in NATO's strategic outlook, underscoring the return of geopolitical competition framed as a confrontation between the democratic West and authoritarian regimes. The annexation demonstrated Russia's capacity to exploit hybrid tactics—integrating military force, disinformation, and economic pressure—to destabilise states without triggering a formal NATO military response under Article 5. This strategy relied on ambiguity, challenging NATO's ability to attribute actions and respond decisively within its traditional and habitual framework.

The Wales Summit Declaration (NATO, 2014a) was NATO's first major policy statement addressing this shift. It highlighted the growing importance of countering hybrid threats, which was described as "a wide range of overt and covert military, paramilitary, and civilian measures are employed in a highly integrated design", designed to undermine societies and erode institutional trust in an "unpredictable world" (NATO, 2014a). This declaration marked a significant broadening of NATO's remit, acknowledging the need to address threats beyond conventional military domains. In a 2014 press conference, NATO Secretary General Jens Stoltenberg articulated this shift, emphasising the Alliance's need to enhance its situational awareness and preparedness: "we are adapting to a changing security environment around NATO. And that's the reason why we are implementing the Readiness Action Plan ... to make our forces more ready, able to deploy at short notice; and also increase our military capabilities. ... And that will also then increase our ability to answer to the threats caused by the idea of hybrid warfare" (NATO, 2014b).

The annexation of Crimea served as a practical demonstration of hybrid tactics in action. Russia's 'little green men', alongside coordinated disinformation campaigns and economic pressure, created a narrative of plausible deniability. NATO, in turn, recognised the need to redefine its strategic responses to encompass these non-traditional threats. In this context, hybrid threats were increasingly framed as existential challenges not only to individual member states but also to NATO's collective identity as a defender of democratic principles as well as peace and stability in Europe (Pindják, 2014).

The 2016 Warsaw Summit Communiqué echoed the same civilisational divide in an increasingly polarised and uncertain world: "There is an arc of insecurity and instability along NATO's periphery and beyond. The Alliance faces a range of security challenges and threats that originate both from the east and from the south; from state and non-state actors; from military forces and from terrorist, cyber, or hybrid attacks" (NATO, 2016b). In such an environment, it was argued that NATO's mission remained unchanged: "to ensure that the Alliance remains an unparalleled community of freedom, peace, security, and shared values, including individual liberty, human rights, democracy, and the rule of law" (NATO, 2016b).

NATO policy briefings from this period reflected a growing concern about the erosion of public trust within member states in an environment of ambiguity and uncertainty, as hybrid threats targeted societal cohesion as much as state institutions. By challenging the credibility of governance and manipulating public discourse, adversaries sought to exploit internal divisions, weakening NATO's ability to present a unified front. Thus, hybrid threats were depicted not only as operational challenges but also as ideological ones, presenting NATO with the responsibility of safeguarding democratic values in an era of asymmetric confrontation.

Characterisation: The West as Defender, the East as Challenger
The Warsaw Summit Communiqué marked a consolidation of NATO's narrative on hybrid threats, situating them within a broader ideological conflict between the democratic West and revisionist actors, particularly Russia. The communiqué framed hybrid warfare as a strategy aimed at undermining the stability of Western democracies and challenging the international order: "Russia's aggressive actions, including provocative military activities in the periphery of NATO territory and its demonstrated willingness to attain political goals by the threat and use of force, are a source of regional instability, fundamentally challenge the Alliance, have damaged Euro-Atlantic security, and threaten our long-standing goal of a Europe whole, free, and at peace" (NATO, 2016b). This characterisation

extended beyond Ukraine, portraying Russia's actions as indicative of a broader strategy to weaken NATO's cohesion. Hybrid tactics, including cyberattacks, electoral interference, and the manipulation of energy dependencies, were depicted as deliberate efforts to exploit vulnerabilities within democratic systems. NATO press materials from 2016 highlighted these challenges, noting the increasing sophistication of hybrid operations and their capacity to blur the boundaries between internal and external threats.

At the same time, NATO's narrative emphasised the resilience of the West. By presenting member states as unified defenders of democracy, NATO sought to counter the perception of vulnerability created by hybrid tactics. This framing served a dual purpose: it reinforced the legitimacy of NATO's role as a security guarantor while also fostering a sense of collective responsibility among member states. In a 2016 speech, NATO Deputy Secretary General Alexander Vershbow stressed this unity: "The final thing we must do is maintain our strong and open societies through our commitment to democracy, human rights and the rule of law. Ultimately, it is our principles, not our military might, that make our societies strong and resilient. And it is those principles which are the surest guarantee we have that, in any confrontation with militarism and adventurism, we will always win out" (NATO, 2016a).

However, NATO's binary framing of hybrid threats as a contest between democracy and authoritarianism risked oversimplifying the dynamics at play. As subsequent NATO documents and briefings recognised, hybrid tactics often exploit domestic weaknesses within democracies themselves, such as political polarisation, economic inequalities, and fragmented media landscapes. This complexity necessitated a nuanced response, balancing traditional deterrence with efforts to address the underlying societal vulnerabilities that hybrid threats seek to exploit.

Emplotment: Institutionalising the Response

The years between 2014 and 2018 were pivotal in shaping NATO's institutional approach to hybrid threats, as the Alliance sought to adapt its identity and mission to an increasingly complex and uncertain security environment. Following Russia's annexation of Crimea, NATO confronted a challenge that blurred the boundaries between military and non-military domains, compelling it to rethink its role as a collective defence organisation. Hybrid threats, which were characterised by ambiguity and a combination of tools to exploit societal vulnerabilities while remaining below the threshold of conventional conflict, posed not only operational but existential questions for NATO. It was within this setting that NATO sought to redefine its relevance in a world where security threats increasingly targeted values, institutions, and cohesion rather than mere physical borders.

The 2014 Wales Summit Declaration provided the first formal acknowledgement of hybrid threats as a central challenge for NATO. By describing hybrid warfare as a tactic designed to destabilise and undermine societies, the declaration implicitly linked these threats to the core principles of democracy and governance that underpin the Alliance. Defining Russia's actions in Ukraine as a "pivotal moment in Euro-Atlantic security", NATO leaders posited that these "have fundamentally challenged our vision of a Europe whole, free, and at peace" with long-term consequences for the security and stability of the region (NATO, 2014a). They reiterated that the Alliance "remains an essential source of stability in this unpredictable world" (NATO, 2014a).

This framing elevated hybrid threats beyond their tactical manifestations, positioning them as strategic challenges to NATO's collective identity. In this narrative, hybrid tactics were not simply operational tools but part of a broader ideological confrontation between the democratic West and revisionist authoritarian regimes. This framing resonated strongly with NATO's foundational purpose, reinforcing its role as a defender of democratic values in a rapidly evolving security environment.

In 2015, NATO formalised its response with the adoption of the Hybrid Warfare Strategy, which sought to integrate hybrid threats into the Alliance's broader defence framework (NATO, 2015). This strategy was a key step in operationalising NATO's evolving understanding of hybrid warfare, prioritising intelligence sharing, situational awareness, and rapid response capabilities. It also highlighted the need for collaboration among member states, recognising that hybrid threats targeted systemic vulnerabilities that transcended national borders. The narrative accompanying this strategy emphasised unity and shared responsibility, particularly with the EU within their 'shared security environment', framing hybrid threats as challenges that required comprehensive, collective solutions (NATO, 2015). By linking hybrid warfare to the concept of collective resilience, NATO began to embed hybrid threats within its long-term strategic outlook.

Institutionalising this narrative culminated in 2017 with the establishment of the Hybrid CoE in Helsinki. The Centre became a symbol of NATO's commitment to addressing hybrid threats as an enduring feature of the security landscape. Its creation underscored NATO's recognition that hybrid threats targeted societal foundations—public trust, critical infrastructure, and economic stability—as much as state institutions. As a result, NATO's response had to extend beyond traditional military domains, integrating civilian capacities and whole-of-society approaches. In this respect, the Centre was presented as a facilitator of cooperation to "help nations and international organisations like NATO and the EU to better understand modern, complex threats and to strengthen our societies against them" (NATO, 2017). Hybrid CoE's mission reflected this shift, reinforcing the narrative that NATO's relevance lay in its ability to adapt and innovate in the face of emerging, multidimensional challenges.

Throughout this period, NATO's evolving response to hybrid threats was tied to its broader narrative of resilience and unity. By framing hybrid tactics as existential threats to democratic values and institutions, NATO positioned itself as more than a military alliance. It cast itself as a central actor in a civilisational struggle, defending the principles of democracy and governance that defined its identity. This narrative bridged the immediate operational challenges of hybrid threats with NATO's long-term vision, embedding these threats within the Alliance's future trajectory while reaffirming its role as a critical guarantor of international stability.

Matured Response: NATO 2030 Agenda (2020) and Strategic Concept (2022)

Setting: Hybrid Threats in an Era of Strategic Competition

The NATO 2030 Agenda and the 2022 Strategic Concept reflected NATO's strategic recalibration in response to an increasingly volatile security environment dominated by strategic competition with authoritarian powers such as Russia and China. These documents marked a significant evolution in NATO's understanding of hybrid threats, situating them within a broader framework of systemic challenges to democratic governance and institutional stability. They outlined the security environment that the Alliance was situated in and defined its priority as "[s]tanding strong together to face a more unpredictable and competitive world" (NATO, 2021a). Highlighting the "contested and unpredictable" nature of the existing order, NATO noted that Russia's war against Ukraine "has shattered peace and gravely altered our security environment" (NATO, 2022, p. 1). Hybrid threats, according to these documents, were no longer ad hoc disruptions but integral components of a sustained strategy by adversaries to undermine the democratic principles that underpin NATO and its member states.

The 2022 Strategic Concept explicitly recognised hybrid tactics as part of a larger, interconnected web of security threats, which included cyberattacks, energy coercion, and information warfare. This framing reflected the understanding that hybrid threats were increasingly sophisticated and multifaceted, targeting both tangible assets—such as critical infrastructure—and intangible foundations, such as public trust in institutions. The emphasis on 'the Western way of life' was particularly significant, linking hybrid threats directly to NATO's identity as the protector of shared democratic values in the face of authoritarian aggression. This narrative drew heavily from the ideological divides that had shaped NATO's Cold War-era identity but updated them for a world where technology, economic interdependence, and transnational challenges had blurred traditional lines of conflict: "Authoritarian actors challenge our interests, values and democratic way of life. They are investing in sophisticated conventional, nuclear and missile capabilities, with little transparency or regard for international norms and commitments. Strategic competitors test our resilience and seek to exploit the openness, interconnectedness and digitalisation of our nations. They interfere in our democratic processes and institutions and target the security of our citizens through hybrid tactics, both directly and through proxies" (NATO, 2022, p. 3).

The broader security environment during this period was also shaped by the ongoing digital transformation, which created both opportunities and vulnerabilities. Digital technologies, while enabling rapid communication and innovation, also provided adversaries with tools to destabilise democracies through cyberattacks, disinformation campaigns, and the exploitation of critical economic dependencies. From the Alliance perspective, these threats aimed at "destabilising our societies and undermining our shared values; and attempts to interfere with our democratic processes and good governance", which required a comprehensive response (NATO, 2021c).

In this context, NATO sought to redefine its mission, positioning itself not only as a military alliance but also as a broader defender of democratic ecosystems within this fractured security order. The NATO 2030 Agenda called for an expanded political role for the Alliance, urging member states to prioritise collective action and resilience against hybrid threats.

Characterisation: A Coordinated Defence of Democratic Systems

NATO's narrative during this period characterised hybrid threats as a coordinated strategy by adversaries to exploit vulnerabilities within democratic systems. These threats, it was argued, sought to erode trust in institutions, destabilise governance, and undermine the rules-based international order. This was portrayed vividly as a clash between two orders: "The rules-based international order, which underpins the security, freedom and prosperity of Allies, is under pressure from authoritarian countries, like Russia and China, that do not share our values. This has implications for our security, values, and democratic way of life. Through the NATO 2030 decisions, NATO will invest in increasing and deepening our partnerships in line with our values and interests to safeguard the rules-based international order" (NATO, 2021a). Hybrid threats were thus presented as systemic challenges that required NATO to adapt its defensive and deterrent strategies beyond traditional military responses.

By targeting public trust, infrastructure, and the media landscape, adversaries aimed to fragment democratic societies, leveraging the same tools of connectivity and globalisation that underpin the Western order. Recognising the interconnected nature of these threats, NATO emphasised unity and collective resilience, framing hybrid threats as challenges that required partnerships across sectors and borders.

A key pillar of this strategy was NATO's deepening cooperation with the EU. EU-NATO collaboration became a cornerstone of the Alliance's response to hybrid threats, leveraging the EU's expertise in regulatory frameworks, economic policy, and cyber governance. The Brussels Summit Communiqué highlighted the importance of this partnership in response to shared threats: "We are working together as an Alliance and with like-minded partners, in particular with the European Union, to protect critical infrastructure, strengthen resilience, maintain our technological edge, and address these challenges to the rules-based international order" (NATO, 2021b). Formalised through the Joint Declarations on NATO-EU Cooperation, this partnership prioritised hybrid and cyber threats as shared challenges. Key initiatives included joint information sharing, exercises, and frameworks for countering disinformation and electoral interference. These agreements reflected NATO's recognition of the EU's regulatory and economic capabilities as critical to countering hybrid tactics as well as a useful ally in defence of the rules-based international order against revisionist powers.

Emplotment: Strengthening Hybrid Resilience Through Partnership

NATO's response to threats during this period revolved around the themes of resilience, partnerships, and innovation. Hybrid threats were framed as a defining challenge of the twenty-first century, requiring not only military solutions but also robust, multidimensional collaboration. This narrative tied NATO's strategic goals to a broader vision of collective security, emphasising the necessity of adaptability and unity in addressing these complex challenges and collaborating with partners, most notably the EU.

One of the key initiatives introduced during this time was the Hybrid Toolbox. Designed to enhance NATO's ability to detect, deter, and respond to hybrid threats, the toolbox provided a flexible framework for integrating capabilities across both military and civilian domains with "comprehensive preventive and response options ... which can be tailored for responding to specific situations" (NATO, 2024b). By leveraging a mix of traditional and emergent capabilities, NATO sought to ensure timely and effective responses to the diverse and interconnected nature of hybrid threats.

Partnerships, particularly with the European Union, became central to NATO's hybrid threat narrative during this period. The collaboration between NATO and the EU deepened significantly, driven by shared concerns over the transnational nature of hybrid threats and the recognition of their impact on both organisations' member states. Joint efforts such as a series of Cyber Coalition collective cyber defence exercises (NATO, 2024a) and emblematic Joint Declarations highlighted the importance of interoperability between the two institutions, allowing them to coordinate responses to hybrid challenges more effectively. In the 2023 Joint Declaration, NATO and EU leaders highlighted the crucial importance of their strategic partnership based on their shared values and "determination to tackle common challenges and ... unequivocal commitment to promote and safeguard peace, freedom and prosperity" (European Council, 2023). Framing the ongoing situation within a strategic competition framework, the declaration noted that the Russian war on Ukraine represented "the gravest threat to Euro-Atlantic security in decades" to undermine peace and stability in the region (European Council, 2023). The partnership between the EU and NATO showcased the complementary roles of NATO and the EU in countering threats of an evolving scope and magnitude (European Council, 2023). NATO contributed its military expertise and strategic coordination, while the EU provided valuable tools for addressing economic and regulatory dimensions. Together, these organisations formed a holistic response framework, combining strengths to address the multifaceted nature of hybrid threats.

Hybrid threats also became a central focus within NATO's broader defence and deterrence strategies. The Strategic Concept of 2022 explicitly outlined plans to embed hybrid threat mitigation into operational planning, ensuring that member states were equipped to address both conventional and non-conventional security challenges (NATO, 2022). This integration signalled NATO's commitment to a comprehensive approach to security, bridging traditional military deterrence with resilience-building efforts across societies.

The narrative of this period reflected a significant shift in how hybrid threats were perceived. No longer seen as mere tactical challenges, they were framed as existential tests of societal resilience and institutional coherence. By fostering partnerships with the EU and other key stakeholders, NATO positioned itself as a central actor in safeguarding democratic values. Its collaborative approach not only strengthened the Alliance's ability to address hybrid threats but also ensured that it remained relevant and adaptive in an era of complex, multidimensional security challenges.

EU Narratives on European Security Through the Leitmotif of Hybrid Threats

Early Days: European Security Strategy (2003) and Global Strategy of the EU (2016)

Setting: A Changing Security Landscape in Times of Crisis

The EU published its second strategy document on its foreign and security policy in June 2016. This bold move on the part of the EU (and its High Representative) came in a difficult period during which the Union was faced with numerous external challenges, alongside the ongoing effects of the Eurozone crisis and the outcome of the British referendum just days prior in its domestic realm. In a period during which the very nature of the integration process was being questioned, the ambitious framework document entitled *Shared Vision, Common Action: A Stronger Europe: A Global Strategy for the European Union's Foreign And Security Policy*—GSEU—set out to (re)define the interests, objectives, and priorities of the Union together with what it stood for in the world. And it did so in a forceful manner. Long gone were the days of the earlier 2003 *European Security Strategy* (ESS), which professed that "Europe has never been so prosperous, so secure nor so free. The violence of the first half of the 20th Century has given way to a period of peace and stability unprecedented in European history" (European Council, 2003, p. 1). In contrast, the 2016 document opened with a pessimistic reading of the current situation: "We live in times of existential crisis, within and beyond the European Union. Our Union is under threat. Our European project, which has brought unprecedented peace, prosperity and democracy, is being questioned" (EEAS, 2016, p. 13). This period, according to the GSEU, was one in which the world has become less secure, its order more fragile, complex, and contested, yet at the same time increasingly interdependent and connected.

The spatial dimension of the EU's conception of its security showed little variation over time: both the ESS and the GSEU, as well as the other documents that followed, talked about the EU as a *global* security actor while containing references to a 'Europe first, the rest of the world second' view of the priorities of the Union. A good example of this line of thinking was provided in the GSEU: "The EU Global Strategy starts at home. … As Europeans we must take greater responsibility for our security. We must be ready and able to deter, respond to, and to protect ourselves against external threats" (EEAS, 2016, pp. 18–19). At the same time, both documents highlighted that distant instabilities, conflicts, and threats indirectly impact the Union's security, compelling the EU to assume global responsibilities and adopt a broader security vision. The ESS, for example, noted that the "traditional concept of self-defence—up to and including the Cold War—was based on the threat of invasion. With new threats, the first line of defence will often be abroad. … Conflict prevention and threat prevention cannot start too early" (European Council, 2003, p. 7). In a similar tone, the GSEU asserted that "our security at home depends on peace beyond our borders. … To promote the security and prosperity of our citizens and to safeguard our democracies, we will manage interdependence … by engaging the wider world" (EEAS, 2016, pp. 7–8).

What changed over the years was the character of the threats and challenges posed to the EU's security and well-being. While the ESS acknowledged that "(l)arge-scale aggression against any Member State is now improbable. Instead, Europe faces new threats which are more diverse, less visible and less predictable", the threats it explicitly identified had more conventional features (European Council, 2003, p. 3). In this respect, while the narrative on threats slowly evolved into the realm of the emergent and elusive, the ESS nevertheless stopped at the threshold and listed the key threats to Europe's security as terrorism, proliferation of weapons of mass destruction, regional conflicts, state failure, and organised crime. The GSEU, however, took the next step towards the realm of unconventional, unpredictable, and evolving threats. While the ESS reflected a post-Cold War, post-9/11 reading of threats that blended internal and external security, the GSEU identified a more complex set of challenges, including existential threats that demanded a strong and collective European response. The GSEU identified hybrid threats—the most elusive and vague of all—alongside terrorism, organised crime, climate change, cyber and energy insecurity, and economic volatility. Although just one of many threats identified, hybrid threats captured the essence of the EU's fragile, complex, and contested security environment, largely due to their fluid and open-ended nature.

Characterisation: Unity as the Foundation of European Security

The EU's response to the changing nature of the international order and its very own 'existential crisis' was to stand even more united in the face of threats and challenges, building on the assumption that its member states are no longer capable of providing the security and prosperity of their citizens on their own: "We need a stronger Europe. This is what our citizens deserve, this is what the wider world expects" (EEAS, 2016, p. 13). As one of the principles guiding the external action of the EU, unity dictated that member states could achieve more together and that "(i)n a more complex world of global power shifts and power diffusion ... (o)nly the combined weight of a true union has the potential to deliver security, prosperity and democracy to its citizens and make a positive difference in the world" (EEAS, 2016, p. 16).

Ultimately, the definitive goal of the EU is to "promote a rules-based global order with multilateralism as its key principle ... to contain power politics and contribute to a peaceful, fair and prosperous world" (EEAS, 2016, p. 15). Achieving this vision is only possible through closer cooperation between the European states on the basis of their shared interests, values, and principles. To this aim, the EU put into action an overarching and comprehensive strategy based on a 'shared vision and common action' to take on the responsibilities expected of it as a "global security provider"

(EEAS, 2016, p. 3). The GSEU went on to explain that the term 'global security provider' was not just a geopolitical reference; it also referred to a wide spectrum of instruments and policies available to the EU. This approach combined elements of soft and hard power, reflecting the idea that "(a) fragile world calls for a more confident and responsible European Union, it calls for an outward- and forward-looking European foreign and security policy" (EEAS, 2016, pp. 4–5). This, in turn, suggests that the EU was concerned with both ontological security—the EU's security "as a particular kind of power"—and physical security as a somewhat limited yet "*sui generis* security provider" (Mitzen, 2006, p. 272; Mälksoo, 2016, pp. 374–375) that functioned on a global level with "a unique mix of tools that no other actor on the global scene has" (Bolvin, 2017).

Emplotment: Hybrid Threats as a Catalyst for European Security Integration

In this period, the notion of hybrid threats garnered increasing attention among EU institutions and bodies, particularly following Russia's involvement in Ukraine and Islamic State's activities outside Syria and Iraq. The increasing salience of the concept led to the creation of several bodies including the Hybrid CoE, the Hybrid Fusion Cell within the European External Action Service,[2] and the European Council's Horizontal Working Party on Enhancing Resilience and Countering Hybrid Threats.[3] In the following period, these bodies produced detailed documents proposing Europe-specific responses to counter hybrid threats.

In its 2016 *Joint Framework on Countering Hybrid Threats*, the European Commission provided a definition of these threats as a "mixture of coercive and subversive activity, conventional and unconventional methods (i.e. diplomatic, military, economic, technological), which can be used in a coordinated manner by state or non-state actors to achieve specific objectives while remaining below the threshold of formally declared warfare" (European Commission, 2016, p. 2). Although the document acknowledged that the definition of hybrid threats "vary and need to remain flexible to respond to their evolving nature", over time it provided a number of useful examples, including disinformation campaigns, and the

[2] The EU Hybrid Fusion Cell is created to gather information and intelligence from member states to inform decision-makers both in EU institutions and in the member states.

[3] The Horizontal Working Party's work primarily focuses on coordinating the European Council's activities on hybrid threats and the resilience of states and societies.

instrumental use of social media to control the political narrative, and the recruitment and radicalisation of proxy actors (European Commission, 2016, p. 2). The report also underscored that hybrid threats aim to exploit the vulnerabilities of the targets, often by seeking to undermine their democratic values and liberties and hindering the decision-making process by creating ambiguity.

To counter these threats, the Commission identified a set of actions to enhance awareness of these threats and to help decision-makers in different spheres to formulate risk-based policies. Key measures included the creation of the Hybrid Fusion Cell to coordinate the activities of the member states in countering hybrid threats and facilitate information and intelligence sharing between them, as well as the Hybrid CoE to promote research on innovative concepts and technologies to counter hybrid threats. Additionally, the Commission highlighted the need to build resilience at different levels and in various sectors to counter these threats, including in critical infrastructure, transportation, and relations with international partners, most notably NATO.

The 2017 "Report on the Implementation of the Joint Framework on Countering Hybrid Threats" was a stocktaking exercise by the Commission that reiterated the fluid, complex, and ubiquitous character of hybrid threats. The Commission assessed the progress of EU-level actions and noted that the ultimate goal of hybrid threats is "to undermine core European values, such as human dignity, freedom and democracy" (European Commission, 2017, p. 2). To counter such threats of an existential nature, the document once again highlighted the need to foster resilience against a wide variety of threats at different levels.

A noteworthy contribution to the debate was provided by the European Parliamentary Research Service in the form of a briefing note. The 2017 Briefing titled "Countering Hybrid Threats: EU-NATO Cooperation" offered a detailed definition of hybrid threats as "a metaphor that captures complexities and dilemmas related to the changing *global environment*. As such, it is a useful concept that *embraces* the **interconnected nature** of challenges (i.e. ethnic conflict, terrorism, migration, and weak institutions); the **multiplicity of actors** involved (i.e. regular and irregular forces, criminal groups); the diversity of **conventional and unconventional means** used (i.e. military, diplomatic, technological)" (European Parliament, 2017, p. 2, emphasis original). This expanded definition illustrated that hybrid threats increasingly function as an umbrella term to refer to a wide spectrum of threats with complex and multidimensional features. These threats now encompass activities ranging from Islamic State operations in Europe to actions by the Turkish government that "used the complexity of migratory movements as a pretext to demand various concessions from the European Union" (European Parliament, 2017, p. 2). This increasingly amorphous character of hybrid threats suggests that the EU—in its quest to ensure both physical and ontological security—transformed its security policy into what is essentially a risk management domain. In this framework, numerous actors at the nation-state and EU levels collaborate to define, assess, and categorise the security environment. Within this environment, the EU—uniquely positioned with both the capacity and the vision for such a leadership role—serves as the central coordinator, guiding the activities of its constituent units and partners.

Strategic Evolution: EU Security Union Strategy (2020) and Strategic Compass for Security and Defence (2022)

Setting: An Era of Strategic Competition and Complex Threats

The 2020 *Security Union Strategy* (SUS) and the 2022 *Strategic Compass for Security and Defence* (SC) are landmark documents framing the EU's approach to an increasingly complex and volatile security environment. They collectively underscore the EU's recognition of the evolving nature of security threats, which challenge traditional distinctions between internal and external security, and demand a coordinated, multilevel response.

A familiar tone regarding the complex security environment of the EU and the multifaceted and novel sources and forms of threats it is faced with dominate the SUS. It is argued in the very introduction that Europe's security landscape is in a state of flux, and the threats to Europe's security have become increasingly complex as a result of global trends such as globalisation and technological and digital transformations. These threats "feed on the ability to work cross-border and on inter-connectivity; they exploit the blurring of the boundaries between the physical and digital world; they exploit vulnerable groups, social and economic divergences" (European Commission, 2020, p. 1).

In this vein, threats in this security environment are defined as constantly evolving, which require the EU to continuously adapt, particularly in view of the wide variety of domains and services that are deemed vulnerable in a global environment that accentuates and multiplies them. In relation to hybrid threats, the SUS highlights the unprecedented scale and diversity of threats the EU faces and notes that while "responsibility for countering hybrid threats lies primarily with Member States", common threats among them, together with their cross-border nature, necessitate "an EU approach to hybrid threats that integrates the external and internal dimension in a seamless flow and brings the national and EU-wide considerations together" (European Commission, 2020, p. 14). Such an EU approach would cover all levels of action, from detection and prevention to response and consequence management (European Commission, 2020, p. 14). Interestingly, in view of the evolving nature of these threats, the SUS also remarks that a particular focus on "mainstream[ing] hybrid considerations into policy making" is required in order to keep up with their pace (European Commission, 2020, p. 14). Referencing "The Landscape of Hybrid Threats"[4]—a policy report published jointly by the European Commission's Joint Research Centre and the Hybrid CoE—it also argued that "[t]he effects of new initiatives will also be assessed through hybrid lenses, including initiatives in areas that have so far been outside the remit of the counter hybrid framework such as education, technology and research" (Commission et al., 2021, p. 15). This is interesting because it opens up the possibility of including anything and everything in the hybrid threat framework. As the Commission notes, "[a]ll policies need a security dimension and the EU can make a contribution at all levels" (European Commission, 2020, p. 20).

The final security concept of the EU—the 2022 *Strategic Compass for Security and Defence* (SC)—opens with an even more pessimistic diagnosis: "**The return of war in Europe, with Russia's unjustified and unprovoked aggression against Ukraine, as well as major geopolitical shifts are challenging our ability to promote our vision and defend our interests.** We live in an era of strategic competition and complex security threats. ... Hybrid threats grow both in frequency and impact" (Council of the European Union, 2022a, p. 2, emphasis original). Building on the first-ever EU Threat Analysis conducted in 2020, a classified document that aims to provide a framework to make sense of the threats and challenges the EU is faced with at the global and regional level, the SC

[4] Interestingly, the report indicated that the term 'hybrid threats' is nothing new. What is new is how threats are "**repackaged and empowered by changing security environment dynamics, new tools, concepts and technologies targeting vulnerabilities in several domains** in an unprecedented manner" (Commission et al., 2021, p. 6, emphasis original).

now adds war to the existing register of security threats thereby signalling the return of power politics and geopolitical rivalry in Europe. The comprehensive security strategy explains that recent geopolitical changes and unjustified Russian aggression against Ukraine crippled the EU's efforts to promote and project its vision and protect its interests. Complex security threats that are of military or non-military nature, sources of instability, and political competition are threatening the existing European security order, and in the face of these challenges, the EU is "showing **an unprecedented resolve to restore peace in Europe, together with** ... [its] **partners**", the most important among them being NATO (Council of the European Union, 2022a, p. 2, emphasis original). Despite this resolve and its former successes in contributing to stability and peace on the European continent, however, the existing security landscape necessitates the EU "**to make a quantum leap forward**" in terms of its willingness and capacity to act as well as its "presence, effectiveness and visibility" at the regional and global level (Council of the European Union, 2022a, p. 2, emphasis original).

Characterising Russia's military aggression against Ukraine as a "tectonic shift in European history", the SC argues that what is at stake today is the existing rules-based international order with multilateralism, human rights and fundamental freedoms, and international law as its key cornerstones (Council of the European Union, 2022a, p. 5). Challenges of a multi-layered nature in multiple theatres, including Syria and Libya, by a revisionist Russia "severely and directly threaten the European security order and the security of European citizens" (Council of the European Union, 2022a, p. 7). The hybrid and conventional tactics and proxies used by Russia render it the primary external threat to be countered in the existing order in Europe. Yet, Russia is not the only state actor that poses a risk to this order. China is also explicitly identified as an 'economic competitor' and 'systemic rival' in the existing rules-based international order (Council of the European Union, 2022a, p. 8).

Characterisation: The EU as a Multidimensional Security Actor

The fact that attacks can come from anywhere, anytime, and in any form without leaving little trace behind rendered the EU a vital actor in the security sphere that is capable of offering a "multidisciplinary and integrated response, helping security actors in Member States with the tools and information they need" and making sure "that security policy remains grounded in ... common European values" (European Commission,

2020, p. 1). In this respect, the EU's contribution to the field of security was deemed crucial as the borders that separated internal from external security disappeared. Every domain and individual became possible targets, highlighting the need for a coordinated approach, particularly with NATO, that functions at multiple levels, starting with the level of human security. Individual member states were deemed no longer capable of protecting their citizens through their actions, and the document argued that "the EU is more prepared and resilient in the first place and has better tools to respond when needed ... [it] has never had more potential to make a difference" (European Commission, 2020, p. 1).

Emplotment: From Fragmentation to Strategic Autonomy
The SC argues that in this period of history, the security of the Union and its citizens is under direct and indirect threats of an unprecedented nature that necessitate 'a common strategic vision' and an urgent, effective, and comprehensive response. The proliferation of threats of all kinds, including those of a hybrid nature, requires the cooperation of all member states under the EU framework at multiple levels and stages, from early detection and prevention to restrictive and recovery measures. As the SC notes, "[t]oday, the EU is surrounded by **instability** and conflicts and faces a war on its borders. We are confronted with a dangerous mix of armed aggression, illegal annexation, fragile states, revisionist powers and authoritarian regimes. This environment is a breeding ground for multiple threats to European security" (Council of the European Union, 2022a, p. 8, emphasis original). For the EU, these threats include "terrorism, violent extremism and organised crime to hybrid conflicts and cyberattacks, instrumentalisation of irregular migration, arms proliferation and the progressive weakening of the arms control architecture" (Council of the European Union, 2022a, p. 8). Strikingly, the EU also notes that "[w]here the EU is not active and effective in promoting its interests, others fill the space" (Council of the European Union, 2022a, p. 8).

To prevent such scenarios and root out the risks associated with them, the EU explains that it relies on its unique combination of capabilities, including the Hybrid Toolbox, Single Intelligence Analysis Capacity, Foreign Information Manipulation and Interference Toolbox, and Cyber Diplomacy Toolbox, to provide a coordinated and comprehensive response. The distinctive contribution that only the EU can provide as a security union in cooperation with NATO is portrayed as vital to regional and global security, as well as the maintenance of the existing rules-based order. In the face of increased use of hybrid tactics by non-state and state actors (particularly Russia) and geopolitical shifts, the EU must equip itself with all the necessary capabilities to "narrow the gap between … [its] aspirations and actions" (Council of the European Union, 2022a, p. 47). The EU's strength, it is argued, "lies in unity, solidarity and determination" as well as strategic autonomy in a security environment in which the borders that separate internal and external security, as well as peace and war, are increasingly blurred (Council of the European Union, 2022b, p. 1).

The war in Ukraine profoundly reshaped the EU's narrative on hybrid threats, sharpening its focus on resilience and the need for unified, decisive action. The use of hybrid tactics by Russia in the lead-up to and during its aggression against Ukraine underscored the strategic utility of hybrid operations in modern warfare. The EU acknowledged that hybrid threats are no longer peripheral but central to destabilising the European security order. In the very introduction to the SC, High Representative Josep Borrell remarked that the crisis in Ukraine "has made it even clearer that we live in a world shaped by raw power politics, where everything is weaponised and where we face a fierce battle of narratives" (Council of the European Union, 2022a, p. 4). In such a setting, he called the EU to action: "We now need to ensure that we turn the EU's geopolitical awakening into a more permanent strategic posture" (Council of the European Union, 2022a, p. 4).

To this end, the EU accelerated its efforts to counter hybrid threats, particularly by enhancing cooperation with NATO. The war in Ukraine also catalysed a significant increase in EU investments in strategic infrastructure and energy independence, addressing vulnerabilities that hybrid threats had previously exploited. By framing hybrid threats as integral to the broader geopolitical competition, the EU positioned itself as a key actor in ensuring the resilience of democratic systems and the rules-based order.

Bibliography

Bertens, H. (2014). *Literary Theory: The Basics* (3rd ed.). Routledge.

Bolvin, J. B. (2017, September 13). *European Union as a Global Security Actor and its Contribution in the GCC and the Middle East*. https://www.eeas.europa.eu/node/32019_en

Chandler, D. (2014). *Resilience: The Governance of Complexity*. Routledge. https://doi.org/10.4324/9781315773810

Commission, E., Centre, J. R., Giannopoulos, G., Smith, H., & Theocharidou, M. (2021). *The Landscape of Hybrid Threats—A Conceptual Model—Public Version* (G. Giannopoulos, H. Smith, & M. Theocharidou, Eds.). Publications Office of the European Union. https://doi.org/doi/10.2760/44985

Council of the European Union. (2022a). *A Strategic Compass for Security and Defence—For a European Union that protects its Citizens, Values and Interests and Contributes to International Peace and Security* (7371/22). https://data.consilium.europa.eu/doc/document/ST-7371-2022-INIT/en/pdf

Council of the European Union. (2022b). *Council Conclusions on a Framework for a Coordinated EU Response to Hybrid Campaigns* (Press Release 603/22).

Duffield, M. (2016). The resilience of the ruins: Towards a critique of digital humanitarianism. *Resilience, 4*(3), 147–65.

Eberle, J., & Daniel, J. (2022). Anxiety Geopolitics: Hybrid Warfare, Civilisational Geopolitics, and the Janus-faced Politics of Anxiety. *Political Geography, 92*(1), 102502. https://doi.org/10.1016/j.polgeo.2021.102502

European Commission. (2016). *Joint Framework on Countering Hybrid Threats* (JOIN(2016) 18 final).

European Commission. (2017). *Joint Report on the Implementation of the Joint Framework on Countering Hybrid Threats—A European Union response* (JOIN(2017) 30 final).

European Commission. (2020). *The EU Security Union Strategy.*

European Council. (2003). *A Secure Europe in a Better World: European Security Strategy.*

European Council. (2023). *Joint Declaration on EU-NATO Cooperation.*

European External Action Service. (2016). *Shared Vision, Common Action: A Stronger Europe, A Global Strategy for the European Union's Foreign and Security Policy.*

European External Action Service. (2018, June 3). *A Europe that Protects: Countering Hybrid Threats.* https://www.eeas.europa.eu/node/46393_en

European Parliament. (2017). *Countering Hybrid Threats: EU-NATO Cooperation* [Briefing].

Galeotti, M. (2022). *The Weaponisation of Everything: A Field Guide to the New Way of War.* Yale University Press.

Hoffman, F. G. (2007). *Conflict in the 21st Century: The Rise of Hybrid Wars.* Potomac Institute for Policy Studies.

Joseph, J. (2013). Resilience as Embedded Neoliberalism: A Governmentality Approach. *Resilience, 1*(1), 38–52. https://doi.org/10.1080/21693293.2013.765741

Joseph, J., & Juncos, A. E. (2019). Resilience as an Emergent European Project? The EU's Place in the Resilience Turn. *JCMS: Journal of Common Market Studies, 57*(5), 995–1012. https://doi.org/10.1111/jcms.12881

Joseph, J., & Juncos, A. E. (2024). Conceptual Politics and Resilience-at-work in the European Union. *Review of International Studies, 50*(2), 373–392. https://doi.org/10.1017/S0260210523000463

Mälksoo, M. (2016). From the ESS to the EU Global Strategy: External Policy, Internal Purpose. *Contemporary Security Policy, 37*(3), 374–388. https://doi.org/10.1080/13523260.2016.1238245

Mälksoo, M. (2018). Countering Hybrid Warfare as Ontological Security Management: The Emerging Practices of the EU and NATO. *European Security, 27*(3), 374–392. https://doi.org/10.1080/09662839.2018.1497984

Mitzen, J. (2006). Ontological Security in World Politics: State Identity and the Security Dilemma. *European Journal of International Relations, 12*(3), 341–370. https://doi.org/10.1177/1354066106067346

NATO. (2014a, September 5). *Wales Summit Declaration issued by the Heads of State and Government Participating in the Meeting of the North Atlantic Council in Wales.* https://www.nato.int/cps/cn/natohq/official_texts_112964.htm

NATO. (2014b, October 1). *Press Conference by Incoming NATO Secretary General Jens Stoltenberg.* https://www.nato.int/cps/en/natohq/opinions_113488.htm

NATO. (2015, December 1). *Press Statements by the NATO Secretary General Jens Stoltenberg and the EU High Representative for Foreign Affairs and Security Policy, Federica Mogherini.* https://www.nato.int/cps/en/natohq/opinions_125361.htm

NATO. (2016a, April 22). *Speech by NATO Deputy Secretary General Ambassador Alexander Vershbow at the Atlantic Club of Bulgaria Conference on Black Sea Security, Sofia.* https://www.nato.int/cps/en/natohq/opinions_130340.htm

NATO. (2016b, July 9). *Warsaw Summit Communiqué Issued by the Heads of State and Government participating in the meeting of the North Atlantic Council in Warsaw 8–9 July 2016.* https://www.nato.int/cps/cn/natohq/official_texts_133169.htm

NATO. (2017, October 2). *Secretary General participates in Hybrid Centre of Excellence inauguration with Finnish leaders and EU High Representative.* https://www.nato.int/cps/en/natohq/news_147497.htm

NATO. (2021a, June). *NATO 2030 Factsheet.* https://www.nato.int/nato_static_fl2014/assets/pdf/2021/6/pdf/2106-factsheet-nato2030-en.pdf

NATO. (2021b, June 14). *Brussels Summit Communiqué Issued by the Heads of State and Government participating in the meeting of the North Atlantic Council in Brussels.* https://www.nato.int/cps/en/natohq/news_185000.htm?selectedLocale=en

NATO. (2021c, June 14). *Strengthened Resilience Commitment.* https://www.nato.int/cps/uk/natohq/official_texts_185340.htm?selectedLocale=en

NATO. (2022). *NATO 2022 Strategic Concept.*

NATO. (2024a). *Cyber Coalition: NATO's Flagship Cyber Exercise*. https://www.act.nato.int/activities/cyber-coalition/#:~:text=Cyber%20Coalition%202023%20took%20place,more%20resilient%20to%20cyber%20threats.

NATO. (2024b, May 7). *Countering Hybrid Threats*. https://www.nato.int/cps/on/natohq/topics_156338.htm

Pindják, P. (2014). Deterring Hybrid Warfare: A Chance for NATO and the EU to Work Together? *NATO Review*. https://www.nato.int/docu/review/articles/2014/11/18/deterring-hybrid-warfare-a-chance-for-nato-and-the-eu-to-work-together/index.html

Sari, A. (2019). The Mutual Assistance Clauses of the North Atlantic and EU Treaties: The Challenge of Hybrid Threats. *Harvard National Security Journal, 10*(2), 405–460.

Umbach, G. (2024). Futures in EU Governance: Anticipatory Governance, Strategic Foresight and EU Better Regulation. *European Law Journal, 30*(3), 409–421. https://doi.org/10.1111/eulj.12519

Williams, M. J. (2009). *NATO, Security, and Risk Management: From Kosovo to Khandahar*. Routledge.

CHAPTER 4

Conclusion: Hybrid Threats, Shared Stories—Narratives of Security in NATO and the EU

The narrative analysis presented here offers a distinct perspective on the role of hybrid threats within the European security framework. By examining the setting, characterisation, and emplotment of NATO and EU narratives, it demonstrates how these institutions construct shared understandings of hybrid threats while advancing their distinct roles in addressing them. The narrative approach reveals the centrality of language and storytelling in shaping perceptions, framing policy responses, and legitimising institutional actions. Hybrid threats are not merely operational challenges; they function as discursive constructs that reinforce institutional priorities and identities, connecting strategic considerations with broader political and ideological dynamics.

Central to this analysis is the role of the leitmotif of hybrid threats, which acts as a unifying thread across the otherwise diverse and complex landscape of European security. The leitmotif serves to integrate multifaceted challenges into a cohesive narrative, creating a shared conceptual framework within which both NATO and the EU operate. By encapsulating the ambiguities and uncertainties of modern security challenges, the notion of hybrid threats enables these institutions to articulate their responses in ways that are adaptable, anticipatory, and wide-ranging. This leitmotif not only legitimises institutional actions but also aligns them with broader ideals of defending democratic values, preserving the rules-based international order, and ensuring societal resilience.

Z. Arkan, *European Security and Hybrid Threats*,
https://doi.org/10.1007/978-3-031-86793-4_4

In terms of setting, hybrid threats are framed as emblematic of a world marked by complexity and unpredictability, where the boundaries between war and peace, internal and external security, and state and non-state actors are increasingly blurred. NATO's focus on the return of civilisational divides and the geopolitical contest between democracy and authoritarianism complements the EU's broader depiction of hybrid threats as systemic risks that pervade economic, social, and technological domains. The leitmotif of hybridity captures this shared context, presenting a security environment in which threats are not isolated incidents but pervasive forces requiring a holistic response.

The characterisation present in security narratives further underscores the importance of the hybrid threat leitmotif. Both NATO and the EU portray themselves as indispensable actors in countering these threats, albeit with distinct emphases. NATO's narrative casts itself as the defender of the democratic West, leveraging military expertise and collective defence to protect against revisionist powers. The EU, on the other hand, positions itself as a multidimensional actor, integrating regulatory, economic, and technological tools to address the full spectrum of hybrid challenges. Despite these differences, the leitmotif of hybridity allows both institutions to present their roles as complementary, forming a unified front against adversaries who exploit ambiguity and systemic vulnerabilities.

In the emplotment of their narratives, NATO and the EU weave hybrid threats into compelling stories that link immediate challenges with long-term strategies. NATO frames hybrid threats as existential tests of societal resilience, requiring collective action and innovation to preserve democratic values and cohesion. The EU, meanwhile, positions hybrid threats as catalysts for integration and strategic autonomy, portraying its multi-level governance framework as uniquely suited to managing complexity. The leitmotif, together with the complementary theme of resilience, serves as the narrative bridge, connecting these storylines and emphasising the interdependence of military, economic, and societal responses.

The war in Ukraine has further reinforced the significance of the hybrid threat leitmotif, demonstrating its relevance even in the context of conventional conflict. While the large-scale violence of the war might seem to overshadow below-threshold activities, hybrid tactics such as disinformation, cyberattacks, and energy coercion have remained central to Russia's strategy. This underscores the persistence of hybrid threats as tools for destabilisation, even amidst broader geopolitical turmoil. NATO and the

EU's narratives have adapted accordingly, integrating hybrid threat mitigation into their broader defence and resilience strategies. The leitmotif thus remained essential, linking the immediate demands of war with the long-term challenges of maintaining societal and institutional stability.

This analysis highlights the profound role of the hybrid threat leitmotif in structuring the European security framework. By providing a unifying narrative, it enables NATO and the EU to articulate their responses to complex and multidimensional challenges in ways that are both cohesive and adaptable. The leitmotif aligns their strategies with broader goals of governance, resilience, and cooperation, ensuring that hybrid threats remain central to their security discourse and practice.

The narrative lens offers a unique contribution to understanding the evolving dynamics of European security. It reveals how hybrid threats, framed as the leitmotif, transcend their technical dimensions to become powerful discursive tools that shape institutional identities, priorities, and actions. The narratives surrounding hybrid threats are not merely about managing risks; they navigate the profound uncertainties of a world marked by complexity, interdependence, and strategic competition. By interweaving NATO and EU narratives, this analysis underscores the pivotal role of hybrid threats in shaping the future of European identity, cooperation, and security governance.

Looking ahead, the NATO-EU partnership's strength will not merely hinge on its ability to adapt to shifting political landscapes but on the narratives crafted to legitimise its relevance. The return of Donald Trump to the presidency raises pressing questions about the transatlantic alliance's stability and, more fundamentally, the dependency on the United States as the guarantor of European security. In an increasingly fragmented geopolitical landscape, NATO and the EU's narrative framing will shape how they balance autonomy and interdependence, but this discourse is far from neutral. The persistent emphasis on resilience and strategic unity risks obscuring the power asymmetries and exclusions embedded within the alliance. Such framing constructs threats as inherently external while legitimising pre-emptive measures and securitisation practices that perpetuate hierarchical relationships. By positioning themselves as the indispensable defenders of democratic values and the rules-based international order, NATO and the EU construct a moral and political superiority that marginalises alternative approaches within the broader security discourse.

Bibliography

Aradau, C., & van Munster, R. (2018). Poststructuralist Approaches to Security. In M. Dunn Cavelty & T. Balzacq (Eds.), *Routledge Handbook of Security Studies* (2nd ed., pp. 75–84). Routledge.

Baele, S. J., & Bettiza, G. (2021). 'Turning' Everywhere in IR: On the Sociological Underpinnings of the Field's Proliferating Turns. *International Theory, 13*(2), 314–340. https://doi.org/10.1017/S1752971920000172

Balzacq, T. (2011). A theory of Securitization: Origins, Core Assumptions, and variants. In T. Balzacq (Ed.), *Securitization Theory: How Security Problems Emerge and Dissolve* (pp. 1–30). Routledge.

Bargués, P., Joseph, J., & Juncos, A. E. (2023). Rescuing the liberal international order: crisis, resilience and EU security policy. *International Affairs, 99*(6), 2281–2299.

Barrett, J. (1996). NATO Reform: Alliance Policy and Co-Operative Security. In I. Peters (Ed.), *New Security Challenges: The Adaptation of International Institutions, Reforming the UN, NATO, EU and CSCE since 1989* (pp. 123–151). St. Martin's Press.

Bertens, H. (2014). *Literary Theory: The Basics* (3rd ed.). Routledge.

Bilgin, P. (2008). Critical Theory. In P. D. Williams (Ed.), *Security Studies: An Introduction* (pp. 89–102). Routledge.

Biscop, S. (2018). *European Strategy in the 21st Century: New Future for Old Power*. Routledge. https://doi.org/10.4324/9780429427442

Biscop, S. (2024). *EU Strategy 2025–2029: We Have the Instruments, Now Set the Objectives* (367; Egmont Policy Brief). Royal Institute for International Relations.

Z. Arkan, *European Security and Hybrid Threats*,
https://doi.org/10.1007/978-3-031-86793-4

Bleiker, R. (2009). *Aesthetics and World Politics.* Palgrave Macmillan.
Bolvin, J. B. (2017, September 13). *European Union as a Global Security Actor and its Contribution in the GCC and the Middle East.* https://www.eeas.europa.eu/node/32019_en
Booth, K. (1991). Security and Emancipation. *Review of International Studies, 17*(4), 313–326.
Bremond, C. (1980). The Logic of Narrative Possibilities (E. D. Cancalon, Trans.). *New Literary History, 11*(3), 387–411. https://doi.org/10.2307/468934
Bribitzer-Stull, M. (2015). *Understanding the Leitmotif: From Wagner to Hollywood Film Music.* Cambridge University Press.
Brubaker, R., & Cooper, F. (2000). Beyond 'Identity'. *Theory and Society, 29*(1), 1–47.
Burgess, J. P. (2012). Introduction. In J. P. Burgess (Ed.), *The Routledge Handbook of New Security Studies* (pp. 1–4). Routledge.
Buzan, B., & Hansen, L. (2009). *The Evolution of International Security Studies.* Cambridge University Press.
Buzan, B., Wæver, O., & Wilde, J. d. (1998). *Security: A New Framework for Analysis.* Lynne Rienner.
Campbell, D. (1998a). *National Deconstruction: Violence, Identity, and Justice in Bosnia.* University of Minnesota Press.
Campbell, D. (1998b). *Writing Security: United States Foreign Policy and the Politics of Identity.* University of Minnesota Press.
Chandler, D. (2014). *Resilience: The Governance of Complexity.* Routledge. https://doi.org/10.4324/9781315773810
Checkel, J. T. (2005). International Institutions and Socialization in Europe: Introduction and Framework. *International Organization, 59*(4), 801–826.
Checkel, J. T., & Katzenstein, P. J. (Eds.). (2009). *European Identity.* Cambridge University Press. https://doi.org/10.1017/CBO9780511806247
Commission, E., Centre, J. R., Giannopoulos, G., Smith, H., & Theocharidou, M. (2021). *The Landscape of Hybrid Threats—A Conceptual Model—Public Version* (G. Giannopoulos, H. Smith, & M. Theocharidou, Eds.). Publications Office of the European Union. https://doi.org/doi/10.2760/44985
Council of the European Union. (2022a). *A Strategic Compass for Security and Defence—For a European Union that protects its Citizens, Values and Interests and Contributes to International Peace and Security* (7371/22). https://data.consilium.europa.eu/doc/document/ST-7371-2022-INIT/en/pdf
Council of the European Union. (2022b). *Council Conclusions on a Framework for a Coordinated EU Response to Hybrid Campaigns* (Press Release 603/22).
Cox, R. W. (1981). Social Forces, States and World Orders: Beyond International Relations Theory. *Millennium: Journal of International Studies, 10*(2), 126–155. https://doi.org/10.1177/03058298810100020501

Crank, J. P., Hoffman, D., & Conn, M. (2008). The 'War on Terror' and Iraq: The Collapse of a Hegemonic Narrative. *Homeland Security Review, 2*(1), 29–56.

Czarniawska, B. (Ed.). (2004). *Narratives in Social Science Research*. Sage.

Dalby, S. (1988). Geopolitical Discourse: The Soviet Union as Other. *Alternatives, 13*(4), 415–442.

Dalby, S. (1992). Security, Modernity, Ecology: The Dilemmas of Post-Cold War Security Discourse. *Alternatives, 17*(1), 95–134. https://doi.org/10.1177/030437549201700104

Darcy, W. (1993). *Wagner's Das Rheingold*. Oxford University Press.

Derrida, J. (1992). *The Other Heading: Reflections on Today's Europe* (P. A. Brault & M. B. Naas, Trans.). Indiana University Press.

Devetak, R. (2009). After the event: Don DeLillo's White Noise and September 11 Narratives. *Review of International Studies, 35*(4), 795–815. https://doi.org/10.1017/S0260210509990192

Diez, T. (2001). Europe as a Discursive Battleground: Discourse Analysis and European Integration Studies. *Cooperation and Conflict, 36*(1), 5–38.

Doty, R. L. (1993). Foreign Policy as Social Construction: A Post-Positivist Analysis of U.S. Counterinsurgency Policy in the Philippines. *International Studies Quarterly, 37*(3), 297–320. https://doi.org/10.2307/2600810

Duffield, J. S. (1994). NATO's Functions after the Cold War. *Political Science Quarterly, 109*(5), 763–787. https://doi.org/10.2307/2152531

Duffield, M. (2016). The resilience of the ruins: Towards a critique of digital humanitarianism. *Resilience, 4*(3), 147–65.

Eberle, J., & Daniel, J. (2022). Anxiety Geopolitics: Hybrid Warfare, Civilisational Geopolitics, and the Janus-faced Politics of Anxiety. *Political Geography, 92*(1), 102502. https://doi.org/10.1016/j.polgeo.2021.102502

European Commission. (2016). *Joint Framework on Countering Hybrid Threats* (JOIN(2016) 18 final).

European Commission. (2017). *Joint Report on the Implementation of the Joint Framework on Countering Hybrid Threats—A European Union response* (JOIN(2017) 30 final).

European Commission. (2020a). *2020 Strategic Foresight Report—Charting the Course towards a More Resilient Europe*.

European Commission. (2020b). *The EU Security Union Strategy*.

European Council. (2003). *A Secure Europe in a Better World: European Security Strategy*.

European Council. (2023). *Joint Declaration on EU-NATO Cooperation*.

European External Action Service. (2016). *Shared Vision, Common Action: A Stronger Europe, A Global Strategy for the European Union's Foreign and Security Policy*.

European External Action Service. (2018, June 3). *A Europe that Protects: Countering Hybrid Threats.* https://www.eeas.europa.eu/node/46393_en

European Parliament. (2017). *Countering Hybrid Threats: EU-NATO Cooperation* [Briefing].

Fisher-Onar, N. (2023). Beyond Binaries: (European) Security in Feminist and Postcolonial Perspective. *European Security, 32*(3), 508–518. https://doi.org/10.1080/09662839.2023.2233436

Foucault, F. (1970). *The Order of Things: An Archaeology of Human Sciences.* Tavistock.

Fukuyama, F. (1989). The End of History? *The National Interest, 16*, 3–18.

Galeotti, M. (2022). *The Weaponisation of Everything: A Field Guide to the New Way of War.* Yale University Press.

George, J. (1994). *Discourses of Global Politics: A Critical (Re)Introduction to International Relations.* Lynne Rienner.

Gheciu, A. (2005). Security Institutions as Agents of Socialization? NATO and the 'New Europe'. *International Organization, 59*(4), 973–1012. https://doi.org/10.1017/S0020818305050332

Gheciu, A. (2019). NATO, Liberal Internationalism, and the Politics of Imagining the Western Security Community. *International Journal, 74*(1), 32–46. https://doi.org/10.1177/0020702019834645

Hansen, A. D., & Sørensen, E. (2005). Polity as Politics: Studying the Shaping and Effects of Discursive Polities. In D. Howarth & J. Torfing (Eds.), *Discourse Theory in European Politics: Identity, Policy and Governance* (pp. 93–116). Palgrave Macmillan. https://doi.org/10.1057/9780230523364

Hansen, L. (2006). *Security as Practice: Discourse Analysis and the Bosnian War.* Routledge.

Hansen, L., & Wæver, O. (Eds.). (2002). *European Integration and National Identity: The Challenge of the Nordic States.* Routledge.

Hill, C. (1993). The Capability-Expectations Gap, or Conceptualizing Europe's International Role. *JCMS: Journal of Common Market Studies, 31*(3), 305–328. https://doi.org/10.1111/j.1468-5965.1993.tb00166.x

Hinchman, L. P., & Hinchman, S. K. (1997). Introduction. In L. P. Hinchman & S. K. Hinchman (Eds.), *Memory, Identity, Community: The Idea of Narrative in the Human Sciences* (pp. xiii–xxxii). State University of New York Press.

Hoffman, F. G. (2007). *Conflict in the 21st Century: The Rise of Hybrid Wars.* Potomac Institute for Policy Studies.

Hoijtink, M., Mühlenhoff, H. L., & Welfens, N. (2023). Whose (in)Security? Gender, Race and Coloniality in European Security Policies: Introduction to the Special Issue. *European Security, 32*(3), 335–346. https://doi.org/10.1080/09662839.2023.2235286

Homolar, A. (2011). Rebels Without a Conscience: The Evolution of the Rogue States Narrative in US Security Policy. *European Journal of International Relations, 17*(4), 705–727. https://doi.org/10.1177/1354066110383996

Huysmans, J. (2006). *The Politics of Insecurity: Fear, Migration and Asylum in the EU.* Routledge.

Hyde-Price, A. (2006). 'Normative' Power Europe: A Realist Critique. *Journal of European Public Policy, 13*(2), 217–234. https://doi.org/10.1080/13501760500451634

Hyde-Price, A. (2007). *European Security in the Twenty-first Century: The Challenge of Multipolarity.* Routledge.

Hyde-Price, A. (2013). Realism: A Dissident Voice in the Study of the CSDP. In S. Biscop & R. G. Whitman (Eds.), *The Routledge Handbook of European Security* (pp. 18–27). Routledge.

Jackson, P. T. (2003). Defending the West: Occidentalism and the Formation of NATO. *The Journal of Political Philosophy, 11*(3), 223–252.

Jørgensen, M., & Phillips, L. (2002). *Discourse Analysis as Theory and Method.* SAGE.

Joseph, J. (2013). Resilience as Embedded Neoliberalism: A Governmentality Approach. *Resilience, 1*(1), 38–52. https://doi.org/10.1080/21693293.2013.765741

Joseph, J., & Juncos, A. E. (2019). Resilience as an Emergent European Project? The EU's Place in the Resilience Turn. *JCMS: Journal of Common Market Studies, 57*(5), 995–1012. https://doi.org/10.1111/jcms.12881

Joseph, J., & Juncos, A. E. (2024). Conceptual Politics and Resilience-at-work in the European Union. *Review of International Studies, 50*(2), 373–392. https://doi.org/10.1017/S0260210523000463

Keohane, R. O., & Nye, J. S. (1977). *Power and Interdependence: World Politics in Transition.* Little.

Kınacıoğlu, M., & Gürzel, A. G. (2013). Turkey's Contribution to NATO's Role in Post-Cold War Security Governance: The Use of Force and Security Identity Formation. *Global Governance, 19*(4), 589–610. https://doi.org/10.1163/19426720-01904007

Klein, B. S. (1990). How the West was One: Representational Politics of NATO. *International Studies Quarterly, 34*(3), 311–325. https://doi.org/10.2307/2600572

Kohler Riessman, C. (2008). *Narrative Methods for the Human Sciences.* Sage.

Kuusisto, R. (2020). *International Relations Narratives: Plotting World Politics.* Routledge.

Libiseller, C. (2023). 'Hybrid Warfare' as an Academic Fashion. *Journal of Strategic Studies, 46*(4), 858–880. https://doi.org/10.1080/01402390.2023.2177987

Linklater, A. (1998). *Transformation of Political Community: Ethical Foundations of the Post-Westphalian Era*. Polity.

Mälksoo, M. (2016). From the ESS to the EU Global Strategy: External Policy, Internal Purpose. *Contemporary Security Policy, 37*(3), 374–388. https://doi.org/10.1080/13523260.2016.1238245

Mälksoo, M. (2018). Countering Hybrid Warfare as Ontological Security Management: The Emerging Practices of the EU and NATO. *European Security, 27*(3), 374–392. https://doi.org/10.1080/09662839.2018.1497984

Mearsheimer, J. J. (1990). Back to the Future: Instability in Europe after the Cold War. *International Security, 15*(1), 5–56. https://doi.org/10.2307/2538981

Mearsheimer, J. J. (2001). *The Tragedy of Great Power Politics*. W.W. Norton & Company.

Mérand, F., Foucault, M., & Irondelle, B. (Eds.). (2011a). *European Security since the Fall of the Berlin Wall*. University of Toronto Press.

Mérand, F., Irondelle, B., & Foucault, M. (2011b). Theorizing Change in the European Security Environment. In *European Security since the Fall of the Berlin Wall* (pp. 3–22). University of Toronto Press.

Merlingen, M. (2012). *EU Security Policy: What It Is, How It Works, Why It Matters*. Lynne Rienner.

Miskimmon, A., O'Loughlin, B., & Roselle, L. (2013). *Strategic Narratives: Communication Power and the New World Order*. Routledge. https://doi.org/10.4324/9781315871264

Mitzen, J. (2006). Ontological Security in World Politics: State Identity and the Security Dilemma. *European Journal of International Relations, 12*(3), 341–370. https://doi.org/10.1177/1354066106067346

Moravcsik, A. (1998). *The Choice for Europe: Social Purpose and State Power from Messina to Maastricht* (0th ed.). Routledge. https://doi.org/10.4324/9781315072258

NATO. (1991). *The Alliance's New Strategic Concept (1991)*. NATO. https://www.nato.int/cps/en/natohq/official_texts_23847.htm

NATO. (2014a, September 5). *Wales Summit Declaration issued by the Heads of State and Government Participating in the Meeting of the North Atlantic Council in Wales*. https://www.nato.int/cps/cn/natohq/official_texts_112964.htm

NATO. (2014b, October 1). *Press Conference by Incoming NATO Secretary General Jens Stoltenberg*. https://www.nato.int/cps/en/natohq/opinions_113488.htm

NATO. (2015, December 1). *Press Statements by the NATO Secretary General Jens Stoltenberg and the EU High Representative for Foreign Affairs and Security Policy, Federica Mogherini*. https://www.nato.int/cps/en/natohq/opinions_125361.htm

NATO. (2016a, April 22). *Speech by NATO Deputy Secretary General Ambassador Alexander Vershbow at the Atlantic Club of Bulgaria Conference on Black Sea Security, Sofia*. https://www.nato.int/cps/en/natohq/opinions_130340.htm

NATO. (2016b, July 9). *Warsaw Summit Communiqué Issued by the Heads of State and Government participating in the meeting of the North Atlantic Council in Warsaw 8–9 July 2016*. https://www.nato.int/cps/cn/natohq/official_texts_133169.htm

NATO. (2017, October 2). *Secretary General participates in Hybrid Centre of Excellence inauguration with Finnish leaders and EU High Representative*. https://www.nato.int/cps/en/natohq/news_147497.htm

NATO. (2021a, June). *NATO 2030 Factsheet*. https://www.nato.int/nato_static_fl2014/assets/pdf/2021/6/pdf/2106-factsheet-nato2030-en.pdf

NATO. (2021b, June 14). *Brussels Summit Communiqué Issued by the Heads of State and Government participating in the meeting of the North Atlantic Council in Brussels*. https://www.nato.int/cps/en/natohq/news_185000.htm?selectedLocale=en

NATO. (2021c, June 14). *Strengthened Resilience Commitment*. https://www.nato.int/cps/uk/natohq/official_texts_185340.htm?selectedLocale=en

NATO. (2022). *NATO 2022 Strategic Concept*.

NATO. (2024a). *Cyber Coalition: NATO's Flagship Cyber Exercise*. https://www.act.nato.int/activities/cyber-coalition/#:~:text=Cyber%20Coalition%202023%20took%20place,more%20resilient%20to%20cyber%20threats.

NATO. (2024b). *Resilience, Civil Preparedness and Article 3*. NATO. https://www.nato.int/cps/en/natohq/topics_132722.htm

NATO. (2024c, May 7). *Countering Hybrid Threats*. https://www.nato.int/cps/on/natohq/topics_156338.htm

NATO. (2024d, October 3). *Relations with the European Union*. https://www.nato.int/cps/en/natohq/topics_49217.htm#:~:text=NATO%20and%20the%20EU%20play,contributes%20to%20transatlantic%20burden%2Dsharing.

Neumann, I. B. (1999). *Uses of the other: 'The East' in European identity formation*. Manchester University Press.

Niemann, A. (2006). *Explaining Decisions in the European Union*. Cambridge University Press. https://doi.org/10.1017/CBO9780511492044

Oppermann, K., & Spencer, A. (2023). Narrative Analysis. In P. A. Mello & F. Ostermann (Eds.), *Routledge Handbook of Foreign Policy Analysis Methods* (pp. 117–132). Routledge. https://doi.org/10.4324/9781003139850-11

Overbeek, H., & Apeldoorn, B. v. (Eds.). (2012). *Neoliberalism in Crisis*. Palgrave Macmillan.

Pindják, P. (2014). Deterring Hybrid Warfare: A Chance for NATO and the EU to Work Together? *NATO Review*. https://www.nato.int/docu/review/articles/2014/11/18/deterring-hybrid-warfare-a-chance-for-nato-and-the-eu-to-work-together/index.html

Ricoeur, P. (1981). Narrative Time. In W. J. T. Mitchell (Ed.), *On Narrative* (pp. 165–186). University of Chicago Press.

Roberts, G. (2006). History, Theory and the Narrative Turn in IR. *Review of International Studies, 32*(4), 703–714. https://doi.org/10.1017/S0260210506007248

Roe, E. (1994). *Narrative Policy Analysis: Theory and Practice.* Duke University Press.

Rogers, J. (2009). From 'Civilian Power' to 'Global Power': Explicating the European Union's 'Grand Strategy' Through the Articulation of Discourse Theory. *JCMS. Journal of Common Market Studies, 47*(4), 831–862.

Rühle, M., & Roberts, C. (2021). Enlarging NATO's Toolbox to Counter Hybrid Threats. *NATO Review.* https://www.nato.int/docu/review/articles/2021/03/19/enlarging-natos-toolbox-to-counter-hybrid-threats/index.html

Rupert, M. (1995). *Producing Hegemony: The Politics of Mass Production and American Global Power.* Cambridge University Press.

Sachseder, J., & Stachowitsch, S. (2023). Gendering EU Security Strategies: A Feminist Postcolonial Approach to the EU as a (global) Security Actor. *European Security, 32*(3), 404–424. https://doi.org/10.1080/09662839.2023.2232742

Sari, A. (2019). The Mutual Assistance Clauses of the North Atlantic and EU Treaties: The Challenge of Hybrid Threats. *Harvard National Security Journal, 10*(2), 405–460.

Schimmelfennig, F. (2003). *The EU, NATO and the Integration of Europe: Rules and Rhetoric.* Cambridge University Press.

Schuman Declaration, May 1950 (n.d.). History of the EU - 1945–59 - Schuman Declaration May 1950. https://europeanunion.europa.eu/principles-countries-history/history-eu/1945-59/schuman-declaration-may-1950_en

Schweller, R. L., & Priess, D. (1997). A Tale of Two Realisms: Expanding the Institutions Debate. *Mershon International Studies Review, 41*(1), 1–32.

Shenhav, S. R. (2006). Political Narratives and Political Reality. *International Political Science Review, 27*(3), 245–262.

Singer, J. D. (1961). The Level-of-Analysis Problem in International Relations. *World Politics, 14*(1), 77–92. https://doi.org/10.2307/2009557

Sloan, S. R. (1986). *NATO's Future: Towards a New Transatlantic Bargain.* Macmillan Press. https://doi.org/10.1007/978-1-349-08362-6

Somers, M. R. (1994). The Narrative Constitution of Identity: A Relational and Network Approach. *Theory and Society, 23*(5), 605–649.

Spencer, A. (2016). *Romantic Narratives in international Politics: Pirates, Rebels and Mercenaries.* Manchester University Press.

Steele, B. J. (2008). *Ontological Security in International Relations: Self-Identity and the IR State.* Routledge.

Subotić, J. (2016). Narrative, Ontological Security, and Foreign Policy Change. *Foreign Policy Analysis, 12*(4), 610–627. https://doi.org/10.1111/fpa.12089

Tocci, N. (with Istituto Affari Internazionali). (2021). *European Strategic Autonomy: What It Is, Why We Need It, How to Achieve It.* Istituto Affari Internazionali (IAI).

Umbach, G. (2024). Futures in EU Governance: Anticipatory Governance, Strategic Foresight and EU Better Regulation. *European Law Journal, 30*(3), 409–421. https://doi.org/10.1111/eulj.12519

Wæver, O. (1989). *Security and the Speech Act: Analysing the Politics of a Word* (Working Paper No. 1989/19). Centre for Peace and Conflict Research.

Wæver, O. (1995). Securitization and Desecuritization. In R. D. Lipschutz (Ed.), *On Security* (pp. 46–86). Columbia University Press.

Wagner, W. (2017). Liberal Power Europe. *JCMS. Journal of Common Market Studies, 55*(6), 1398–1414. https://doi.org/10.1111/jcms.12572

Wallace, W. (2017). European Foreign Policy Since the Cold War: How Ambitious, How Inhibited? *The British Journal of Politics and International Relations, 19*(1), 77–90. https://doi.org/10.1177/1369148116685297

Wallander, C. A. (2000). Institutional Assets and Adaptability: NATO After the Cold War. *International Organization, 54*(4), 705–735. https://doi.org/10.1162/002081800551343

Waltz, K. N. (1979). *Theory of International Politics.* Addison-Wesley.

Waltz, K. N. (1993). The Emerging Structure of International Politics. *International Security, 18*(2), 44–79.

Weber, C. (2010). *International Relations Theory: A Critical Introduction* (3rd ed.). Routledge.

Weldes, J., Laffey, M., Gusterson, H., & Duvall, R. (1999). Introduction: Constructing Insecurity. In J. Weldes, M. Laffey, H. Gusterson, & R. Duvall (Eds.), *Cultures of Insecurity: States, Communities, and the Production of Danger* (pp. 1–33). University of Minnesota Press.

Wendt, A. (1994). Collective Identity Formation and the International State. *American Political Science Review, 88*(2), 384–396. https://doi.org/10.2307/2944711

White, H. (1981). The Value of Narrativity in the Representation of Reality. In W. J. T. Mitchell (Ed.), *On Narrative* (pp. 1–23). University of Chicago Press.

White, H. (1987). *The Content of the Form: Narrative Discourse and Historical Representation.* Johns Hopkins University Press.

Whitney, C. R. (1991, January 25). War in the Gulf: Europe; Gulf Fighting Shatters Europeans' Fragile Unity. *The New York Times.*

Wigell, M. (2019). Hybrid Interference as a Wedge Strategy: A Theory of External Interference in Liberal Democracy. *International Affairs, 95*(2), 255–275. https://doi.org/10.1093/ia/iiz018

Williams, M. J. (2009). *NATO, Security, and Risk Management: From Kosovo to Khandahar*. Routledge.

Wyn Jones, R. (2001). Introduction: Locating Critical International Relations Theory. In R. Wyn Jones (Ed.), *Critical Theory and International Politics* (pp. 1–19). Lynne Rienner.

Yurdusev, A. N. (1993). 'Level of Analysis' and 'Unit of Analysis': A Case for Distinction. *Millennium: Journal of International Studies, 22*(1), 77–88. https://doi.org/10.1177/03058298930220010601

Index

Z. Arkan, *European Security and Hybrid Threats*,
https://doi.org/10.1007/978-3-031-86793-4